The Campus History Series

TULANE UNIVERSITY

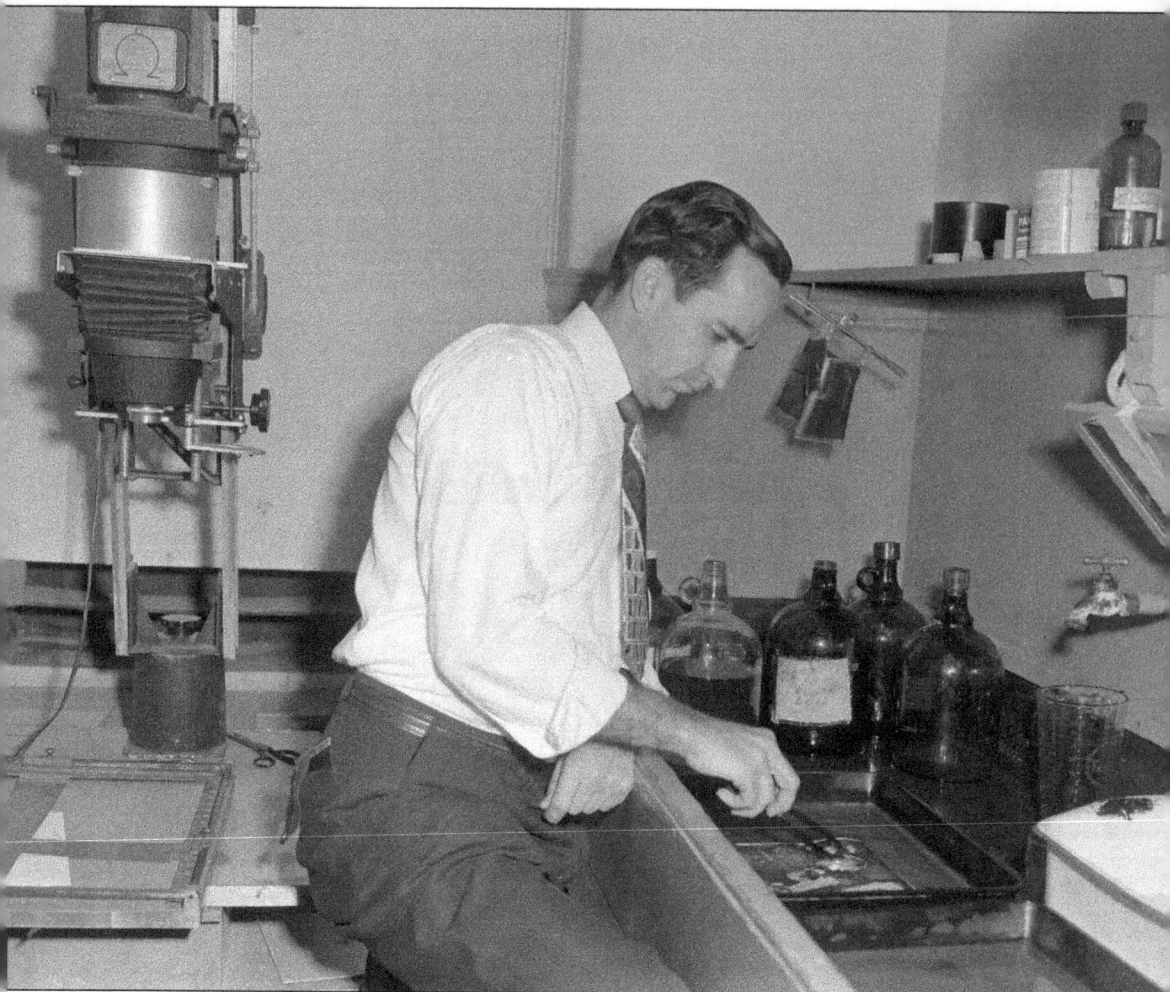

Armand Bertin was the university photographer at Tulane from 1947 to 1989. He shot almost every event, group, game, and individual at the university for 40 years and is credited with the majority of the images in this book. (Tulane University Archives.)

ON THE COVER: The 1929–1930 cheerleading squad had plenty to yell about. Under coach Bernie Bierman, the 1929 football team was unbeatable, going 9-0 in one of only three perfect seasons in Tulane football history. The cheering squad of, from left to right, Frank Chalaron, Clinton Arnold, Bruno Stolley, Gladys Matthews, and C.A. Allenburger kept the crowds in sync when chanting the "Hullabaloo." In the background image, Tulane Stadium is seen during the Tulane vs. Louisiana State University football game on December 2, 1933. The game was played to a 7-7 tie. (Tulane University Archives.)

The Campus History Series

TULANE UNIVERSITY

ANN E. SMITH CASE

ARCADIA
PUBLISHING

Published by Arcadia Publishing
Charleston, South Carolina

Library of Congress Control Number: 2015954744

For all general information, please contact Arcadia Publishing:
Telephone 843-853-2070
Fax 843-853-0044
E-mail sales@arcadiapublishing.com
For customer service and orders:
Toll-Free 1-888-313-2665

Visit us on the Internet at www.arcadiapublishing.com

For my father; and for those who have gone before.

CONTENTS

ACKNOWLEDGMENTS

When I decided to undertake the challenge of writing this pictorial history, it was to do just that—to write a history that would be illustrated with some of the great images in our collections, rather than just assemble a photographic album of historical snapshots. My first acknowledgment must be that, even after studying and working at Tulane for the past 34 years, I still learn something new (or old) about this place every day.

Most of the information in this book is drawn from documentation contained within the Tulane University Archives, the repository of the university's historical records. Portions of these documents have been variously interpreted in several published histories of Tulane. Contemporary newspaper accounts have provided additional details. Unless otherwise noted, all images come from the archives. Any errors or faulty conclusions are solely my own.

The photographic collection is comprised of images either curated or created for use in university publications, with the majority of images shot between 1947 and 1989 by staff photographer Armand Bertin. In the 1990s, Jerry Ward and others took photographs that may appear in these pages. Since 1999, Paula Burch-Celentano has been the primary university photographer; works by other photographers included herein are annotated.

Several other Tulane University repositories contributed images to this book, for which I am extremely grateful. Mary Holt at the Rudolph Matas Library of the Health Sciences (RMLHS) and Chloe Raub of the Newcomb Archives and Vorhoff Library (NAVL) generously scanned items in their collection and granted permission to use them. Gena Chattin, digital archivist in the Office of Editorial and Creative Services, gave me the keys to the digital kingdom of images too modern for my archives—many thanks.

Sincere appreciation goes to my Special Collections director, Bruce Raeburn, and library dean (now retired) Lance Query for their strong support of this project. Likewise, this project would never have begun without the initial support of executive vice president for university relations and development Yvette Jones and vice president for university communications and marketing Deborah Grant.

I relinquish the title of household curmudgeon back to my husband, Mike Case, with gratitude for his patience these past four months.

Penultimate acknowledgements are given to my "ad hoc advisory committee," Katheryn Warzak, Lori Schexnayder, and Jeff Rubin, who gave me advice when, like an optometrist, I asked them, "which do you like better, this one, or this one . . . this one, or this one . . . ?" I would also like to thank my colleagues in Special Collections for their support. My editor, Liz Gurley, has made this process as painless as possible.

Finally, heartfelt apologies to all of the Tulanians whose team, club, dormitory, project, discipline, favorite faculty member, building, or activity I couldn't fit into this short history. Please refer to the digitized yearbooks and other material available through the University Archives website, tuarchives.tulane.edu, to augment your cherished memories. Roll Wave!

INTRODUCTION

In 1834, the ancestor of Tulane University was created out of adversity, and 171 years later, Tulane emerged out of the floodwaters of Hurricane Katrina and recreated itself into the vibrant, forward-thinking university that it is today. This is a story of transformation from a small, local college into an international research institution whose roots have always been grounded on the premise of service to the public.

The institution now known as Tulane University was founded as the Medical College of Louisiana by a group of young doctors in 1834. Although they had no resources other than their medical training, these men proposed the formation of a medical college in the city of New Orleans, a thriving port town periodically besieged by yellow fever and cholera epidemics, because it was sorely needed in a region that had no formal means of educating physicians.

The private Medical College of Louisiana became the public University of Louisiana in 1847, offering classes in medicine, law, literature, and the natural sciences. Forty years later, wealthy businessman and philanthropist Paul Tulane was inspired to help educate the male youths of the city; with his donation, the university again became private and in 1884 was renamed the Tulane University of Louisiana. Following his lead, Josephine Louise Newcomb established the H. Sophie Newcomb Memorial College as a department within Tulane University in 1886; this was the first coordinate women's college in the nation.

Originally situated in downtown New Orleans near its Charity Hospital, the Medical College of Louisiana/University of Louisiana/Tulane University outgrew its physical facilities as the 19th century waned, necessitating a division of the university onto separate campuses by academic units. On the cusp of the 20th century, a new campus for Tulane's undergraduate students was opened in uptown New Orleans, five miles from the medical campus, which remained downtown. These two campuses—a downtown medical campus and an uptown undergraduate campus—still remain the nucleus of Tulane University today.

Newcomb College was also initially located downtown, on Tivoli (Lee) Circle, before moving to the Garden District five years later. Newcomb spent almost 30 years on this campus, developing its unique identity. This was the birthplace of the famed Newcomb Pottery Enterprise, which offered women a chance to contribute to their own livelihoods by learning a variety of crafts.

During the 20th century, the undergraduate colleges united on one campus and matured in all aspects of collegiate life. Tulane's curriculum expanded to include the Schools of Architecture, Commerce, Dentistry, and Public Health. Real-world events such as World War I, the Spanish influenza epidemic, and World War II reached onto campus and, in turn, pulled the university's constituents back out into the world.

Tulane's football team garnered national attention, earning two invitations to the Rose Bowl and inspiring the New Orleans Mid-Winter Sports Association to establish the Sugar Bowl. In the inaugural game on January 1, 1935, which was played on Tulane's campus, Tulane beat Temple 20-14. The immediate and continued success of the classic bowl game led the City of New Orleans to finance the enlargement of Tulane Stadium several times, resulting in a stadium that eventually held 80,000 fans—enough to encourage the NFL to award a professional football franchise to the city.

The second half of the 20th century brought intense social change on campus, as the student population changed from local to national to international and from predominantly white to diverse. Politically-inspired events such as the Kent State tragedy led to an increase in student activism, protests, sit-ins, and even the burning of a military barracks on Tulane's campus. National headlines were made when Pres. Gerald Ford announced the end of the Vietnam War while giving an address at Tulane.

Tulane was chosen to host a regional primate research center, at which researchers made critical discoveries regarding AIDS, tuberculosis, and Lyme disease. Downtown, Tulane medical faculty merged excellence in teaching with innovation in discovery, pioneering in heart surgery, physiology, endocrinology, and pharmacology; twice, faculty members won the Nobel Prize.

Then came the storm that changed everything.

Hurricane Katrina hit New Orleans on August 29, 2005; the resulting damage forced the university to close for the fall semester. Along with much of Tulane's physical facilities, the floodwaters that rose during the aftermath also washed away the university's existing academic structure. Faced with unprecedented physical damage to repair and potential fiscal losses in the millions, the administration made the decision to restructure its academic organization in order to achieve greater integration and synergy among related disciplines. The Renewal Plan eliminated various programs, departments, and schools, and put greater emphasis on science and subjects related to the transformation of urban communities.

Renewed and redefined according to its historical strengths—its world-class educational programs and its relationship to the city of New Orleans—Tulane would move forward, focused on the holistic development of undergraduates in a campus-centric environment.

Committed to helping rebuild the city of New Orleans, Tulane instituted an undergraduate public service graduation requirement. In doing so, it followed in the steps of the Tulane Law School, which became the first law school in the country to require pro bono service in 1987.

Academic and administrative initiatives, both within the walls of the university and out in the greater community, proved to be successful in rebuilding financial stability and creating collaborative ties with its neighbors.

In mid-September 2005, Tulane physicians began providing free medical care for New Orleans citizens in clinics throughout the city. On February 14, 2006, Tulane University Hospital and Clinic reopened, the first hospital to reopen in downtown New Orleans since Katrina.

Tulane City Center (TCC) was created in November 2005 as the primary venue for outreach projects at the School of Architecture. Combining consultation and design services and following through with on-site construction, faculty and students collaborated with low-income groups and nonprofit organizations to help revitalize New Orleans neighborhoods. In its first decade of operation, TCC completed 80 projects across the city, such as the Grow Dat Youth Farm.

Mandated by the Renewal Plan, the Tulane Center for Public Service was established in August 2006. As part of new curricular requirements for graduation, students integrated community service with academic projects throughout their years at Tulane. By 2015, the university offered over 280 service-learning courses that enrolled more than 3,000 students and represented 62,000 service hours contributed each year.

In December 2006, the Scott S. Cowen Institute for Public Education Initiatives was founded with a grant from the Lavin Family Foundation. Named for Tulane's president, who served as chair of the Education Committee of the Bring New Orleans Back Commission, the center focused on improving the New Orleans public education system. It has continued to operate as a think tank, issuing, among other reports, the annual *State of Public Education in New Orleans*.

In the 10 years since Katrina, Tulane has made a remarkable recovery, physically and in spirit. Enrollment numbers are the highest in the school's history. Financial losses of $650 million have been mitigated by $425 million in recovery dollars. A new president, Michael A. Fitts, has stepped into the leadership position, ready to guide the university by focusing on collaboration and innovation. A top-level global research institution, Tulane is the largest private-sector employer in the city of New Orleans. As such, it takes its responsibility to the people of New Orleans to heart. Whether it be through providing services in health care, architecture, public service, or education, the Tulane family truly strives to embody the university's motto, *Non Sibi Sed Suis*—not for one's self, but for one's own.

One

BEGINNINGS
1834–1890s

Seeing the desperate need for trained physicians in the city of New Orleans, seven doctors—
Thomas Hunt, Charles A. Luzenberg, John H. Harrison, Thomas R. Ingalls, Augustus H.
Cenas, J. Monroe Mackie, and Edwin B. Smith—announced their intention to establish the
Medical College of Louisiana by publishing their prospectus in *L'Abeille* (The Bee), the local
bilingual newspaper, on September 29, 1834.

This was the beginning of the institution now known as Tulane University. These seven
doctors, without any mandate other than the firm belief of its necessity, began to educate
others to help their fellow man. The Medical College of Louisiana operated as a private
institution from 1834 until 1847, at which time it was incorporated into the newly formed,
state-legislated University of Louisiana as its Medical Department.

Lack of state funding, lack of proper elementary education, and regular epidemics of yellow
fever and cholera combined to keep enrollments low at the University of Louisiana. Fortunately
for the citizens of New Orleans, generous donors such as Paul Tulane and Josephine Louise
Newcomb came forward in the 1880s to provide a much-needed infusion of capital to further
the educational opportunities of the young men and women of the city.

Paul Tulane was a wealthy philanthropist from New Jersey who had made his fortune as a
businessman in New Orleans. He donated his extensive real estate holdings in New Orleans
to establish the Tulane Educational Fund, to be controlled by a board of administrators who
could either create a new university or foster an existing one. These worthy advisors, led by
Randall Lee Gibson, agreed to foster the floundering University of Louisiana, thus creating
the Tulane University of Louisiana in 1884.

Born in Maryland, Josephine Louise LeMonnier Newcomb was a wealthy widow who had
lived only a small portion of her life in New Orleans prior to her gift. After the death of her
daughter Harriott Sophie from diphtheria at the young age of 15, she was inspired in 1886 to
establish the H. Sophie Newcomb Memorial College within the Tulane University of Louisiana
as the country's first coordinate women's college.

When the prospectus for the Medical College of Louisiana (MCL) was published in 1834, the only other institution of higher education in the city was the College of Louisiana, with 66 students. Most of the medical colleges in the country were located in northern states, with only Georgia and South Carolina conferring degrees upon physicians in the South. Medical training for students consisted of two four-month sessions of lectures at the college and one year of apprenticeship with a practicing physician. Eleven students matriculated the first year.

With no facilities, equipment, or library of its own, the new institution opened on January 5, 1835. Thomas Hunt (pictured), founder and first dean of the MCL, delivered the inaugural lecture in a hall offered by Dr. Theodore Clapp's Congregational church. Tickets were sold to anyone who wished to attend. For students, the total cost of attending college was about $140 per year; this covered the cost of purchasing tickets to each professor's lecture series, $20 paid directly to each faculty member, plus the matriculation and graduation fees, which the dean collected. Each lecture series lasted about four months.

10

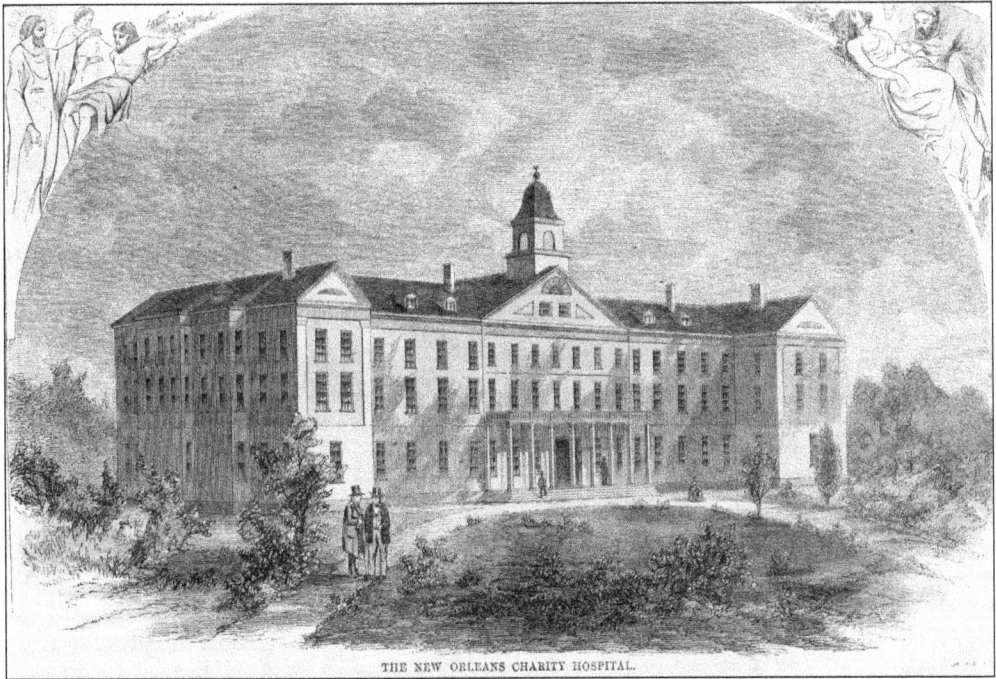

THE NEW ORLEANS CHARITY HOSPITAL.

To relieve the space crunch in the face of growing enrollment numbers, the faculty rented out space at 41 Royal Street and held classes at faculty members' homes. In 1836, the faculty resolved to serve the state-owned Charity Hospital (pictured) free of charge, and was permitted to give lectures in one of its rooms. Generations of Tulane physicians trained within Charity Hospital walls, serving as interns and as physicians. The cooperative arrangement between the university and Charity Hospital lasted until Hurricane Katrina closed the doors to Charity permanently. (RMLHS.)

As the chair of the Chemistry Department beginning in 1836, John L. Riddell taught at the university for 29 years. He was also chair of Materia Medica and Therapeutics beginning in 1839, when the university awarded its first pharmacy degree. An accomplished field botanist, geologist, science lecturer, numismatist, and politician, he garnered international attention with his invention of the binocular microscope in 1852. He served as smelter and refiner at the US Mint and postmaster general of New Orleans during the Civil War.

11

Tired of operating out of borrowed and rented spaces for so many years, in 1843, the faculty leased from the state a plot of ground upon which it erected the first permanent facility for the college, a three-story Greek Revival edifice located on Common Street near Charity Hospital. The college professors provided free service to Charity Hospital for a period of 10 years and offered one free scholarship per parish as chosen by the legislature. Dr. Isidore Labatut donated his personal medical library, but the faculty had to pay for journals out of its own pockets.

At the Louisiana State Constitutional Convention in 1845, the legislature was authorized to create a state university, albeit one with little financial support. Its act of February 1847 provided that the Medical College of Louisiana would become the Department of Medicine of the University of Louisiana, thus creating a public institution with a minimal amount of state funding. In addition to medicine, the University of Louisiana was designed to provide education in the law, letters, and natural sciences.

Rev. Dr. Francis Lister Hawks was named the first president of the University of Louisiana. In 1847, he was rector of the Christ Episcopal Church in New Orleans. Educated at the University of North Carolina and at Yale, Hawks spent 10 years practicing law before entering the Episcopal ministry. Although he resigned the presidency after just one year, worn down by the stress of running a university without financial support, he was convinced to stay for an additional two years.

In the initial rush of enthusiasm for the University of Louisiana's creation, the legislature appropriated $40,000 for a new building for the Medical Department, which would soon outgrow its four-year-old building given the expansion of the university's new educational offerings. When finished, the Medical Department occupied the large center and east wings of the new building, ceding its original building, now called the west wing, to the Law Department.

1, West Wing.   2, Central Building.   3, East Wing

UNIVERSITY OF LOUISIANA.

1, Law Department   2 & 3, MEDICAL DEPARTMENT

On Common St. bet. Baronne and Dryades Sts. N. O.

In establishing the first successful law school in Louisiana, four faculty members were appointed to teach civil, common, admiralty, and constitutional law: Judge Henry Adams Bullard, Richard Henry Wilde, Judge Theodore Howard McCaleb (pictured), and Randell Hunt. Twenty-three students enrolled for the 1847–1848 academic session. Tuition was $100 per year, and lectures were given in the courtroom of the customhouse in the afternoons and evenings. There were 16 graduates at the end of the first year.

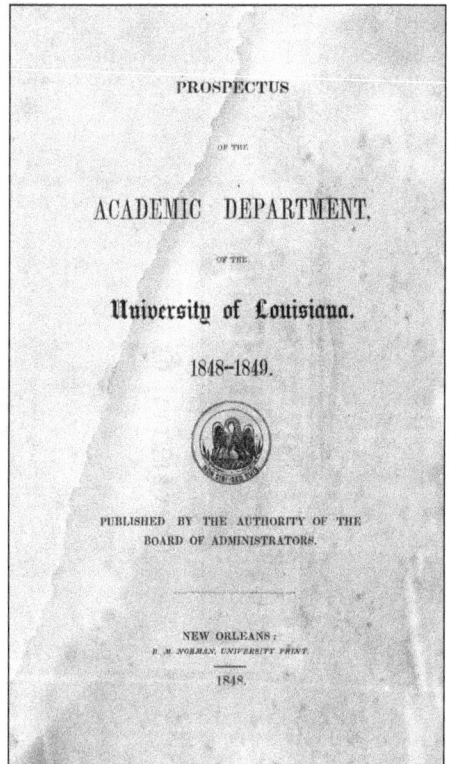

PROSPECTUS

OF THE

ACADEMIC DEPARTMENT,

OF THE

University of Louisiana.

1848–1849.

PUBLISHED BY THE AUTHORITY OF THE
BOARD OF ADMINISTRATORS.

NEW ORLEANS:
B. M. NORMAN, UNIVERSITY PRINT.

1848.

In anticipation of populating a collegiate department for instruction in letters and natural sciences, a preparatory school called the Academic Department was established in the east wing of the campus. Forty students matriculated the first year, taught by five faculty members. After enough students had progressed academically, the Collegiate Department opened in 1851 with 12 freshmen and two sophomores. The first bachelor's degrees were awarded in 1857, to Joseph Arsenne Breaux (bachelor of arts), Charles Gaudin (bachelor of science), and William Valloft (bachelor of science).

Because financing was slow in coming from the state, the University of Louisiana depended heavily upon donors. Judah Touro, Glendy Burke, Louis Bush, and Maunsel White were generous donors in the earliest days; their gifts helped to keep the university open. The Glendy Burke Medal for Elocution and the Touro Medal for Ancient History were among prized honors to be earned. Endowed accounts in these names still exist, and awards continue to be given annually. (Ann Case.)

The Civil War closed the doors to the University of Louisiana for four long years. While the city was occupied by Union forces, space was given in the west wing to the Abraham Lincoln School for Freedmen, seen here, and in the east wing to the New Orleans Academy of Science. Both groups had to be evicted in 1866, when classes finally resumed after the war. Fortunately for the University of Louisiana, the Reconstruction government actually provided for the maintenance and support of the university in the constitution of 1864—on paper, anyway.

THE "ABRAHAM LINCOLN SCHOOL" FOR FREEDMEN, NEW ORLEANS, LOUISIANA.—[PHOTOGRAPHED BY LILIENTHAL, NEW ORLEANS.]

15

After the Civil War, only the Medical and Law Departments reopened. Agricultural and mechanical education were seen as imperative for the South's recovery, so state legislators forced it upon the University of Louisiana in 1874, moving an agricultural and mechanical college into its east wing. Not pleased with having this interloper underfoot, the medical faculty was relieved when the college moved upriver to join Louisiana State University in Baton Rouge a few years later. This event spurred the University of Louisiana to reopen its own Academic Department in 1878, pictured here. Tuition was $50 per year.

Born in Bonnet Carré, Louisiana, to well-educated Spanish parents, Rudolph Matas (standing, second from left) enrolled in medical school at age 17 and immediately became indispensable. His fluency in Spanish enabled him to act as assistant and interpreter to Dr. Stanford Chaillé (seated, second from right, facing camera) in Cuba while they investigated causes for yellow fever in 1879. Chaillé, a pioneer in public health, later became dean of the medical school. (RMLHS.)

16

Paul Tulane

Paul Tulane moved to New Orleans from New Jersey at the age of 21, a young man with merchandising skills and financial backing from his father. Within a short time, Paul Tulane and Company was a well-known firm specializing in wholesale and retail sales of clothes, hats, and shoes. Tulane never married, had no heirs, and eventually moved back to New Jersey. After a lifetime of success, the wealthy philanthropist contacted Randall Lee Gibson, offering to donate parcels of real estate to finance an educational institution for young men in New Orleans. Tulane's Act of Donation was dated July 10, 1882. Although no formal ceremony was held, the painting below portrays the moment of the donation.

Randall Lee Gibson, a state representative and alumnus of the University of Louisiana (bachelor of law, 1855), suggested that a board of advisors or administrators be appointed to guide the expenditure of the fund. The first Board of Administrators of the Tulane Education Fund was composed of 17 respected men of the community, drawn from a variety of bankers, lawyers, clergymen, educators, and businessmen. Gibson was named the first president of the board.

With Act 43 of 1884, the financially struggling University of Louisiana officially became the Tulane University of Louisiana. In consideration of the agreement of the board to develop and maintain the University of Louisiana, the act provided tax-exempt status in perpetuity. It also created free legislative scholarships, one from each senatorial and representative district in the state, that are still being awarded each year.

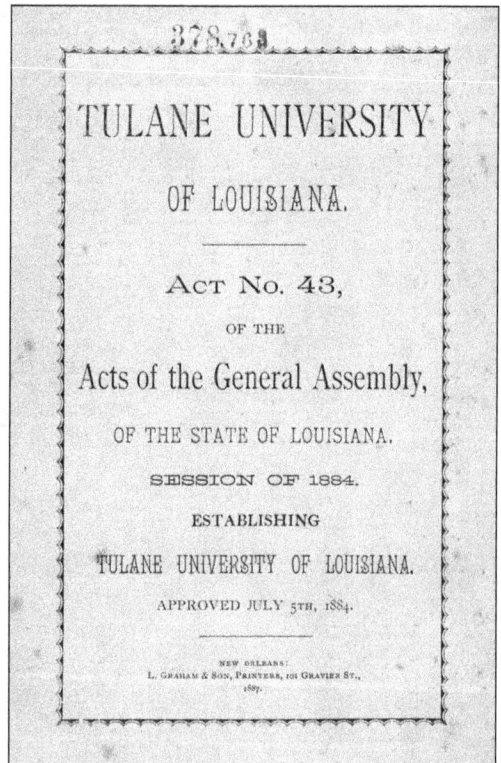

378.763

TULANE UNIVERSITY

OF LOUISIANA.

ACT No. 43,

OF THE

Acts of the General Assembly,

OF THE STATE OF LOUISIANA.

SESSION OF 1884.

ESTABLISHING

TULANE UNIVERSITY OF LOUISIANA.

APPROVED JULY 5TH, 1884.

NEW ORLEANS:
L. GRAHAM & SON, PRINTERS, 101 GRAVIER ST.,
1887.

William Preston Johnston was hired
to be the first president of Tulane
University, taking him from that same
role at Louisiana State University.
When asked his goals for the new
university, he outlined a threefold
approach: to educate the youth,
to provide a community-oriented
program of adult education, and to
develop knowledge through hands-
on research conducted in scientific
investigations in laboratories. Both
Tulane and Johnston believed that
technological education was needed
in the South at this time. Johnston's
goal was for an education that both
informed and trained.

In 1881, the board of
administrators purchased
the Mechanics Institute
building, located around
the corner from campus,
to obtain more classroom
space for the Academic
Department. In exchange
for waiving the back
taxes, the mayor was
allowed to nominate five
city scholarships each
year. It was renamed
Tulane Hall after Paul
Tulane paid off the
mortgage. When Tulane
College relocated to the
uptown campus in 1894,
the Law Department
occupied Tulane Hall.

TULANE MANUAL TRAINING BUILDING.

Turners' Hall, at the corner of Lafayette and Dryades Streets, was bought to house the dynamos and other large pieces of mechanical equipment needed for Prof. John Morse Ordway's manual training classes. By day, this building was the workshop for the Tulane High School. At night and on Saturdays, Turners' Hall became a community center where adults gathered for free classes in drawing, mechanics, shorthand, public health, French literature, electricity, and magnetism that were offered by the university from 1885 to 1894. The drawing classes were extremely popular with both men and women, with over 4,700 registrants over the nine years that they were offered. The success of this adult education program laid the groundwork for University College in later years.

Josephine Louise Newcomb, wealthy widow of Warren Newcomb, suffered the unspeakable tragedy of losing her only daughter, Harriott Sophie, at age 15. Sophie, born in 1855, was said to have had strength of character and sweetness of disposition unusual for someone of her age. To honor her daughter, Mrs. Newcomb established an institution of higher learning for the education of girls and young women of New Orleans, the H. Sophie Newcomb Memorial College, in 1886. This was the country's first coordinate college, created as a department within and under the administration of Tulane University. Mrs. Newcomb's gifts to the college eventually totaled over $3.6 million. (NAVL.)

Brandt V.B. Dixon was hired to be the first president of Newcomb College. He was an inspired choice as steward for Newcomb. He would spend 32 years forming the college and acting as the conduit between Josephine Louise Newcomb and the board of administrators. Ultimately, Dixon was Newcomb's only president; after Newcomb joined Tulane on its uptown campus, the administration of the women's college was placed under a dean rather than a separate president to help unify the colleges into a single institution.

The first campus building for Newcomb was this brownstone on the corner of Camp Street and DeLord Street (now Howard Avenue) in downtown New Orleans. It had three large rooms for classrooms on the lower floor, a parlor for an assembly room and chapel, and seven rooms upstairs for classes. Across a large backyard, there was a smaller two-story brick building that held the scientific laboratories.

Josephine Louise Newcomb's desire was that her memorial college would look to the practical side of life as well as to literary excellence. Like Tulane College, Newcomb College needed to offer preparatory or high school coursework in addition to its collegiate literary, scientific, and industrial art and design curriculum. In 1887–1888, the first year of classes, there were 59 students registered in academic classes, at $100 in tuition, and 91 students registered as special students and art students, at $40 tuition.

TULANE UNIVERSITY OF LOUISIANA.

ANNOUNCEMENT OF

H. SOPHIE NEWCOMB MEMORIAL COLLEGE.

1887-'88.

The H. Sophie Newcomb Memorial College is founded upon an endowment made by Mrs. Josephine Louise Newcomb, of New York City, the widow of Warren Newcomb, formerly a highly esteemed merchant of New Orleans. Mrs. Newcomb vested this endowment in the administrators of the Tulane Educational Fund, in the full confidence of their ability and fidelity in the administration of so important a trust. Her design is the establishment of an institution for the higher education of white young women and girls, which, while it looks to solid learning, shall yet afford opportunities for practical and industrial studies. The institution is intended to supplement, not to interfere with, the excellent female schools in this city, and is to be Christian, but not sectarian. By act of the administrators it is established as a department of Tulane University.

It is the aim of this College to offer to the young women of Louisiana and the adjoining States a liberal education, similar to that which is now given to young men by the Tulane University, and to young women also by other institutions of the first rank in distant parts of the United States.

The last few years have witnessed an extraordinary impulse in the cause of female education elsewhere; colleges similar to this have sprung up in various localities, and have been filled to overflowing; whilst in our own community the increasing desire that such an enterprise should be undertaken has arisen to an imperative demand.

To meet these educational needs, a system of instruction has been devised, which is believed to be liberal, thorough and specially adapted to the prevailing conditions. The Faculty has been carefully selected for their ability and fitness.

In 1885, Ellsworth Woodward joined his older brother, William, on the faculty at Tulane to teach fine arts. When Newcomb College was established, he was named the head of its School of Art. Professor Woodward advocated for occupations in fine handicrafts and the arts, establishing the Newcomb Pottery Enterprise in 1895 and incorporating programs in arts and crafts, such as drawing, painting, needlework, bookbinding, and silverwork into the curriculum.

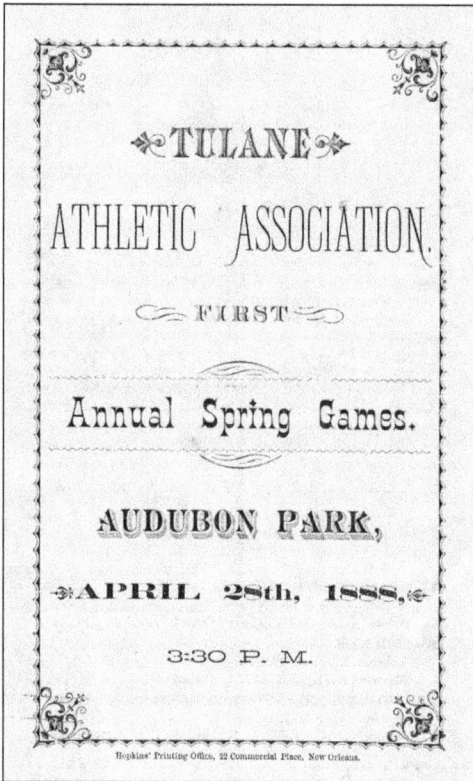

TULANE

ATHLETIC ASSOCIATION.

FIRST

Annual Spring Games.

AUDUBON PARK,

APRIL 28th, 1888,

3:30 P. M.

Hopkins' Printing Office, 22 Commercial Place, New Orleans.

With no athletic facilities of their own, students traveled uptown to Audubon Park to stage their first intramural athletic competition, the Spring Games, in 1888. Events included running and hurdle races, shot put, broad jump, high jump, high kick, and the baseball throw. Winners received either a gold or a silver medal. The first intercollegiate track competition that Tulane attended was in 1894, with Tulane winning every event it entered.

On November 18, 1893, Tulane's new football team faced the Southern Athletic Club in Sportsman's Park, an athletic field in mid-city New Orleans, and was beaten 12-0. The following week, the "Tulanes" beat their rivals from upriver, Louisiana State University, 34-0 in a game that had an estimated attendance of 2,000. Tulane adopted the team colors and nickname "Olive and Blue," beginning with the December 2, 1893, game against the University of Mississippi.

Two

GROWTH AS AN INSTITUTION
1890s–1945

The end of the 19th century brought changes to all of the departments of Tulane University. Enrollment numbers rose drastically in the Medical Department, despite stricter admissions standards and graduation requirements. New facilities were made possible through the generosity of new donors. Two new schools were created within the medical field, the Dental Department (1909) and the School of Hygiene and Tropical Medicine (1912).

Newcomb College experienced a similar growth, albeit more slowly in enrollment numbers. The college moved from its downtown location to the Garden District in 1891, spending 28 years as a Southern female college somewhat isolated on its own campus before moving to join Tulane on its Broadway campus in 1919. These years of operating essentially as a self-contained unit were critical for the development of the Newcomb spirit of independence.

Tulane College also made an exodus from downtown New Orleans, moving to 18 acres in uptown New Orleans in 1894. To better represent its educational philosophy, the board of administrators also split Tulane College into the College of Arts and Science and the College of Technology. New curricula were added within the university as well, with an architecture degree being offered in the College of Technology (1908) and the establishment of the College of Commerce and Business Administration (1914) and the School of Social Work (1927).

When America declared war on Germany in 1917, the effects were felt on campus immediately. Tulane students took military training and Newcomb students formed the Newcomb Relief Unit. Ultimately, 75 percent of the faculty was involved in wartime training or in active service, and more than a thousand alumni saw active service.

Tulane experienced a period of expansion after the war, tripling the endowment thanks to a development program spearheaded by Pres. Albert Dinwiddie. Some of this growth can be credited to the success of the intercollegiate athletics program, most visibly the tennis teams and the football teams, which played in a Rose Bowl and two Sugar Bowl games between 1932 and 1940. School spirit also flourished, with an official alma mater and team nickname being formalized.

The Naval ROTC scholarship program that began in 1938 became a precursor to the V-12 program that operated on campus during World War II. Once again, Tulane answered the call of duty.

Richardson Memorial, located on Canal Street, was the second home of the Medical Department. Built in 1893 as a memorial to Dr. Tobias G. Richardson, it was twice the size of the former facility, having four floors that housed lecture and recitation rooms and laboratories for chemistry, pharmacy, practical anatomy, operative surgery, pathology, and bacteriology. The building was renamed the Josephine Hutchinson Memorial in 1906 after a donation from Alexander Charles Hutchinson.

The typical day's schedule was for the students to accompany professors on clinical rounds and attend lectures in Charity Hospital from 8:30 a.m. to 12:00 p.m. each morning, then return to Richardson Memorial for didactic lectures after the clinics. Requirements for graduation were strengthened in 1893 to include three full years of medical coursework; laboratory work in bacteriology, chemistry, and operative surgery; a thesis on a medical subject; and successfully passing examinations before members of the faculty.

The library was located on the first floor of Richardson Memorial, along the east side of the building in a wing with a reception room, coatrooms, and dean's and other professors' offices. The library had been generally neglected before Ida Richardson's donation but was admirably reestablished, with the first librarian, Jane G. Rogers, hired to administer the library during the academic year. By 1897, there were about 3,400 bound volumes in the library, with a monthly patron use count of about 250.

The microscopy laboratory on the second floor of Richardson Memorial was designed so that its 84 microscopes could take full advantage of sunlight coming through the windows. In 1895, it was thought to be the largest, best ventilated, and best lit laboratory in the country. Required coursework in microscopical bacteriology and anatomy was taught by Dr. P.E. Archinard, a pupil of Louis Pasteur.

The contents of the Museum of Anatomy, on the top floor of Richardson Memorial, were acquired in 1850, when the university had been appropriated $25,000 by the state to purchase anatomical slides and apparatus. Two faculty members went on a shopping spree in Europe to buy wax copies of musculature preparations in Italy, bones and other osteological specimens, and specimens of skin and eye diseases in France.

Practical anatomy was an optional course in the 1880s, offered five nights a week under the tutelage of a demonstrator. The fee for taking the course was only $10, half that of a regular medical course, even though the demonstrator performed basically the same duties as a professor: directing dissection, reviewing other professors' notes as they pertained to related anatomical topics, and asking and answering questions for the students. He did not have to secure the subjects for dissection; evidently, the janitor took care of that duty.

Throughout its existence, the university's medical instruction included training at the nearby Charity Hospital. When the elite Ambulance Corps was organized in 1885, the best third- and fourth-course medical students were allowed to take competitive examinations to be chosen for a two-year appointment as residential intern. While on ambulance duty, each intern would treat all emergency cases and answer all ambulance calls. This photograph shows Charity Hospital ambulance interns and house surgeons around 1905.

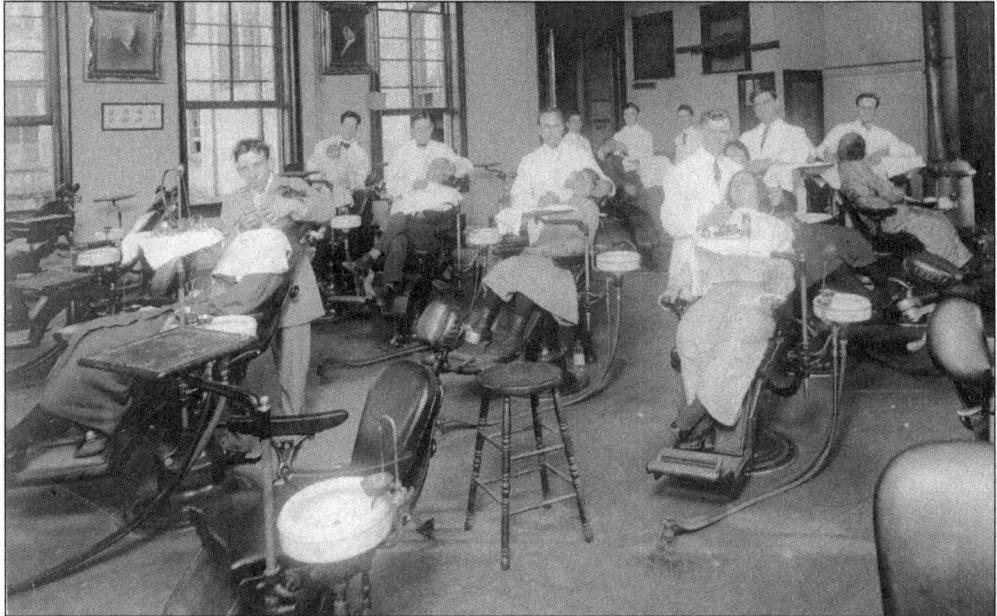

The New Orleans College of Dentistry was officially organized in 1899 as an institution independent from Tulane, but within a decade, it had become the Dental Department of Tulane University. Women were allowed to enroll under the same terms and conditions as men, a privilege not extended to women who wished to register for classes in the Medical Department. A free dental clinic was open daily to the general public.

By 1890, Newcomb had outgrown its small downtown campus, so it purchased the three-acre Burnside Place estate, a whole block bounded by Washington, Camp, Sixth, and Coliseum Streets, for $45,000. Burnside had been built by railroad magnate James Robb, and it had been lavishly furnished; extensive remodeling was necessary to convert the main house into Newcomb Hall. A second floor was added in order to create enough classroom space as well as to add a chapel and assembly room. This photograph was taken around 1899.

Newcomb Hall was ready for occupancy in 1891. This octagonal mirrored hall, a holdover from the Robb House, was used as a Reception Room. The art studios and chapel were located upstairs initially, before separate buildings for those functions were erected in 1893. In the first year at this locale, Newcomb College had 63 registered regular students, 21 special students, 32 art students, and 42 high school students.

The class of 1891 decided that their colors, bronze and blue, would be the official colors for Newcomb College. This was also the inaugural year for many events that would become important traditions in the Newcomb experience: May Day, Spring Arts Festival, Little Commencement, and Gym Night. Pi Beta Phi sorority was the first sorority to be established on campus, also in 1891; Kappa Kappa Gamma was established in 1904.

Newcomb alumnae traditionally have been involved in keeping the Newcomb spirit alive after the commencement speeches were finished. The Newcomb alumnae began a loan fund, financed through an annual alumnae show, and they organized a Newcomb Alumnae Free Night School in 1905, offering classes three times a week from 7:00 to 9:00 p.m. They had this room to use as a meeting place within Newcomb Hall.

Constructed in 1894, Josephine Louise House was built to serve as a dormitory at Newcomb College. Students were allowed to go out at night only on Friday evenings, and lights-out was at 10:15 p.m. For several years, Josephine Louise Newcomb occupied room number 1 when she visited New Orleans; however, the noise generated by the more active younger women finally compelled her to buy a house on nearby Fourth Street, where she became a permanent resident.

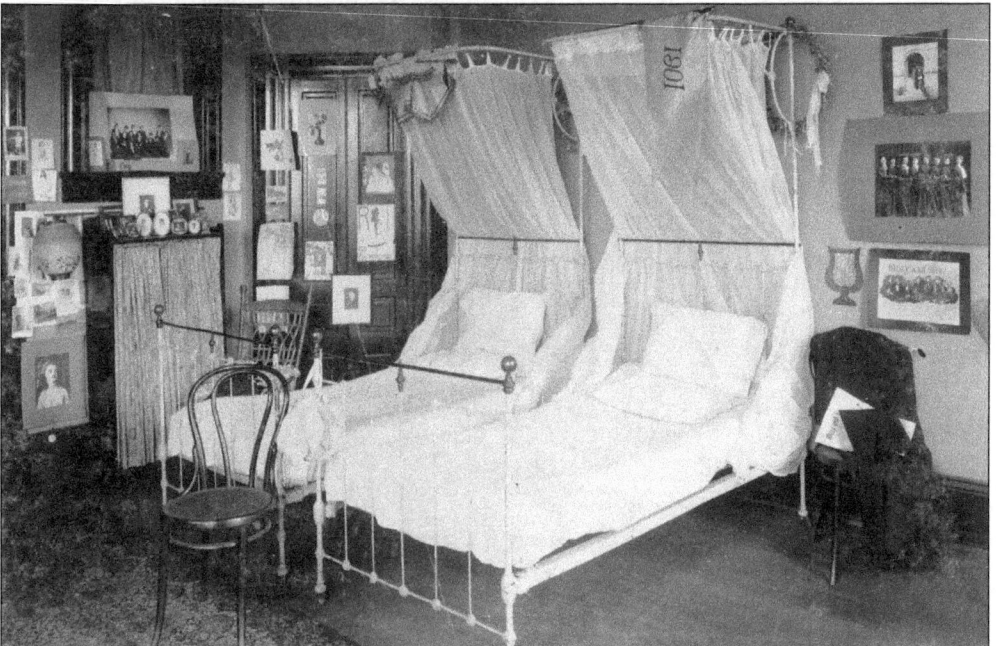

In 1901, the cost of board and lodging was $180 per year to share a double and $225 for a single in Josephine Louise House. Each student needed to provide her own linens, towels, and mosquito netting. This room housed a Newcomb senior; her cap and gown are draped across the chair, and photographs on the walls show her classmates in their senior attire.

The coursework for Newcomb students was very similar to that of the Tulane students with regard to the natural sciences. During their four years of undergraduate studies, students in both schools were required to take classes in physics, biology, astronomy, geology, chemistry, French, and German. The physics laboratory is being used here around 1901. The laboratories were located in the Academy, a second classroom building that was adjoined to Newcomb Hall by the two-story Arcade.

Chemistry was a required course for every student, no matter which course of study was being pursued, because it was seen as a necessary building block for understanding nutrition, home economics, domestic science, and the properties of food. Specialized chemistry courses were also implemented for more targeted studies, such as ceramic chemistry and organic chemistry.

The popularity of the free drawing classes translated into a high demand for the art classes at Newcomb, with regular and special students taking classes in painting, sketching, and watercolor. This life class was held on the second floor of Newcomb Hall. By 1894, a separate building had been erected for art coursework, and a four-year curriculum had been established in the School of Art.

Ellsworth Woodward, director of the Newcomb School of Art, was well-known in New Orleans for hosting an annual December show. He was one of the founders of the New Orleans Art Association and was active in the Southern States Art League. He taught at Newcomb for 46 years before retiring in 1931. Here, he instructs a class of mostly senior Newcomb art students in still life painting.

34

The Newcomb Pottery was established in 1894, when Mary Given Sheerer arrived from Cincinnati to teach ceramic decoration. Pieces were thrown by Joseph Meyer, at right above, and decorated by Newcomb student artists using local flora and fauna motifs. The Newcomb Pottery enterprise, which operated from 1895 to 1940, was given a great boost when Newcomb pottery won a bronze medal at the Paris Exposition in 1900; ultimately, eight medals were won in international exhibitions before 1916. During the 45 years of its operation, the enterprise produced nearly 70,000 distinctive pieces of pottery and provided employment to 90 Newcomb graduates. The pottery showroom, adjacent to the studio, displayed shelves of the pieces, which are still very collectible. Desiree Roman, the first art graduate from Newcomb, is shown below in the pottery sales room.

In 1909, Newcomb opened a Department of Household Economy, which offered classes in dietetics; food and its preparation; the chemistry and bacteriology of food; the comparative value of foods; domestic arts such as dressmaking, millinery, and embroidery skills; and household decorating. Household management, which included marketing and keeping accounts, was also part of the curriculum, as were the ubiquitous courses in education, physical education, chemistry, biology, and art.

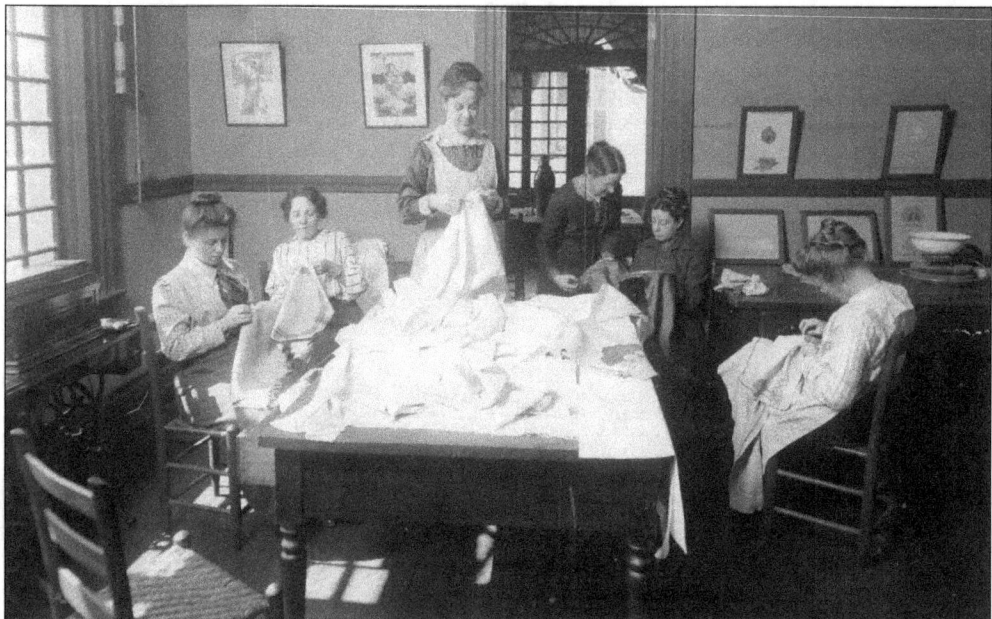

Embroidery was introduced into the school in 1902, according to a Newcomb brochure, as a means of expressing art into function. Because the handicraft required no special apparatus or extra expenditure, it was seen as a branch of art that should be a profitable and limitless form of self-expression that epitomized the idea of "art as applied to industry." Standing are Amelie Roman, left, and Gertrude Roberts Smith, right.

Clara Gregory Baer was the indefatigable physical education teacher at Newcomb College from 1891 to 1929. She originated and designed the department, starting the discipline's first teacher certification program and four-year degree program in the South. She is best known for authoring in 1896 the first book of rules for women's basketball and for inventing the game "Newcomb," akin to volleyball, which is still played in summer camps across the country.

In the Baer version of basketball, or basquette, the objective was to score a goal by passing the ball down the court between teammates and throwing it into a netted hoop. Each player was paired with a defender, and each pair was restricted to one of seven small zones on the court. Two-handed passes were not allowed, as that was thought to compress the chest. Dribbling, guarding, talking, and snatching the ball were not allowed.

By 1893, Tulane College had grown too large for its Common Street campus downtown. The administrators purchased 18 acres of land in the uptown suburbs of New Orleans on which they would situate their new campus. Four units were erected in 1894: the Arts and Sciences Building, the Physical Laboratory, the Chemical Laboratory, and a building complex housing mechanical and electrical laboratories, drawing rooms, and workshops. The Medical Department remained in its downtown location, as did the Law Department.

This imposing four-story building constructed out of Bedford limestone was the focal point of the new campus. Named the Arts and Sciences Building, it housed the offices of the board of administrators, the president, and the secretary; the library; a faculty room; an assembly hall; classrooms for arts and sciences coursework; offices for the professors; the Linton-Surget Art Gallery; the museum; and a gathering room for the students. Designed by the firm of Harrod and Andry, its architectural style is Richardsonian Romanesque. The building was renamed Gibson Hall after Randall Lee Gibson, first president of the board of administrators.

The New Orleans Academy of Sciences gifted its collection of paleontological and zoological specimens to the university to join the Ward collection of minerals and other natural history specimens that had been acquired through a Paul Tulane donation. Other collections included the Gustave Kohn group of Louisiana fauna, the George Soule collection of mammal skeletons, and the Joseph Jones collection of reptiles. The University Museum was housed in the top floor of Gibson Hall until it was dispersed in 1957.

The Linton-Surget Art Collection, containing books, painting, statuary, and objets d'art, was bequeathed to the City of New Orleans in 1889 by Mary Surget. Placed under the perpetual charge of Tulane's board, the collection was displayed on the third floor of Gibson Hall. It formed the nucleus of what is now known as the Tulane University Art Collection.

Gibson Hall's basement has served many nonacademic functions. It was an early site for canteen service, offering cream cheese and ham sandwiches for a nickel. At one point, it housed a bookstore and a post office. In 1915, an indoor range for .22-caliber rifle practice was installed for the Tulane Rifle Club. It was also the site of the first student center on campus, shown here in 1904.

Alcée Fortier began his association with the university as principal of the preparatory department of the University of Louisiana in 1880, then became professor of French, and ultimately served as professor of Romance languages until his death in 1914. A noted linguist specializing in Louisiana Creole and Acadian French dialects, he was a standard fixture in the Arts and Sciences Building. Fortier Hall was named in his honor.

The Physical Laboratory, left, sat on the western boundary of the campus, whereas the Chemical Laboratory, front right, the Mechanical and Electrical Laboratories, the workshops for the mechanical arts, and the powerhouse lined the eastern boundary. The quadrangle closest to the academic buildings was left as greenspace, and the back area was allotted for athletic fields. An observatory was added by 1901.

In 1898, the first radio transmission ever completed in the South from one building to another was sent from a set built in the Physical Laboratory. The feat was accomplished by seniors A. Baldwin Wood and William Monroe White. In this photograph of the advanced physics laboratory, Wood holds a speaker to his ear. Despite their pioneering efforts in wireless telegraphy, both men's career paths lay in hydraulic engineering.

Graduates of Newcomb College, or female graduates of other accredited colleges with an undergraduate or master's degree, could take graduate-level classes offered on the Tulane campus. In this photograph, a female biology graduate student is making use of a microscope in her studies, while Dr. George Beyer is instructing Percy Viosca in the center of the room. The first female to receive an advanced degree in biology from Tulane was Laura Alice McGloin in 1904.

The Chemistry and Physical Laboratories were modeled on laboratories at other universities like Cornell and Vanderbilt. The ceilings were made of varnished wood so that no particles of plaster could fall and contaminate chemicals being used in experiments. Likewise, the walls in the laboratories were lined with enameled or pressed bricks.

Practical training in mechanical arts such as foundry work and forging was available through the College of Technology, which, along with the College of Arts and Sciences, was formed out of the old Collegiate Department when Tulane University moved to its uptown site. In 1920, the College of Technology was renamed the School of Engineering. In this college, foundry work, forging, pattern-making, tool-making, and drawing were required of all freshmen and sophomores. The ratio of coursework was one to two hours of lecture per week to six hours of hands-on training. There were 30 forges and an equal number of anvils and sets of blacksmith's tools available in the foundry (above) and blacksmith shop (below).

All freshmen and sophomores in the College of Technology were also required to take courses in carpentry (above) and machine-tool work (below), in addition to academic classes in English, algebra, geometry, chemistry, history, mechanical drawing, rhetoric, and either French, German, or Spanish. The broad scope of academic coursework was intended to provide students with historical, linguistic, and philosophical knowledge so that in addition to being trained for leadership in industrial activity, they would be men of culture. During the junior and senior years, coursework became more specialized towards the course of study: electrical, mechanical, civil, chemical, sugar engineering, or architectural engineering.

The uptown campus was built on 18 acres of the Foucher tract, a former sugar plantation. Given the importance of the sugar industry in Louisiana, it is not surprising that a sugar chemistry degree was offered within the College of Technology beginning in 1897. Special coursework entailed industrial chemistry classes, plus work with sugar house machinery, steam boilers, and chemical control of the sugar house. The degree was discontinued in 1915. In the chemical laboratory above, a student grinds a sugar stalk to extract its juice while classmates perform other tests. Below, Prof. Levi Wilkinson directs his students how to plant sugarcane into furrows just beyond the chemistry building.

Land surveying was one part of the civil engineering coursework; here, students practice in the campus green between the observatory and the water tower. Other aspects of the civil engineering curriculum included railroad and highway engineering, graphic analysis of stresses in wind load and in masonry structures, bridge and roof trusses, hydraulics, construction, and masonry construction.

Eugene Delery, left, and A.B. Davis, center, are learning astronomical concepts under the tutelage of Dr. Brown Ayres, dean of the College of Technology and professor of physics, astronomy, and electrical engineering. These two 1899 civil engineering graduates stayed in New Orleans and contributed to the workforce as engineers with the Sewerage and Water Board and Levee Board.

The Electrical Engineering Laboratory provided the opportunity for interactive learning for, from left to right, T.M. Logan, A. Baldwin Wood, and John S. Harris. Wood later designed and installed the huge screw pumps that continue to drain the streets of New Orleans today. His sloop *Nydia* was displayed on Tulane's campus until 2003, when it was removed for restoration. In 2009, *Nydia* was returned to the Wood family, and is currently on display in Biloxi at the Maritime and Seafood Industry Museum.

In 1884, William Woodward joined the Tulane faculty, hired to teach mechanical and architectural drawing. Educated at the Rhode Island School of Design, he taught the collegiate, high school, and free drawing classes for men and women. He was the faculty chairman of the committee to build the Tilton Memorial Library, and in 1907, he organized the Department of Architecture. Later in life, he became known for documenting buildings in the Vieux Carré (French Quarter).

Tulane had its own printing press, originally located in the attic of the Physical Laboratory. Students could earn spending money by helping to print and assemble college catalogs, circulars, stationery, and other publications. Tulane University Press was in operation from 1899 to 1961, and its original Optimus Cylinder press was still in working order when the office finally closed its doors.

Although it was preceded by the *Tulane Rat* (1890–1892), the first newspaper to be printed with any longevity was the *College Spirit*, published weekly on Wednesdays from 1894 to 1897. Edward Rightor, class of 1895, was the editor, and a yearly subscription cost $1. Each issue ran four pages, and it advertised a directory for all of the official organizations of the college: the athletic association; the games committee; football, baseball, and tennis teams; the mandolin and banjo club; the glee club; the Glendy Burke Literary Society; fraternities; and the *Tulane Collegian*, a bimonthly publication that began in 1892.

The first dormitory on campus was built in 1902, the same year as the neighboring refectory cafeteria (now Cudd Hall) and Tilton Library (now Tilton Hall). The three-story building, most recently known as the Social Work Building, was divided into three sections named La Salle, Bienville, and Gayarré. Each house held 16 rooms configured in pairs with shared study areas. The cost to lodge here was anywhere from $3 to $8 per month, depending on how many roommates shared the rooms and which floor the student occupied.

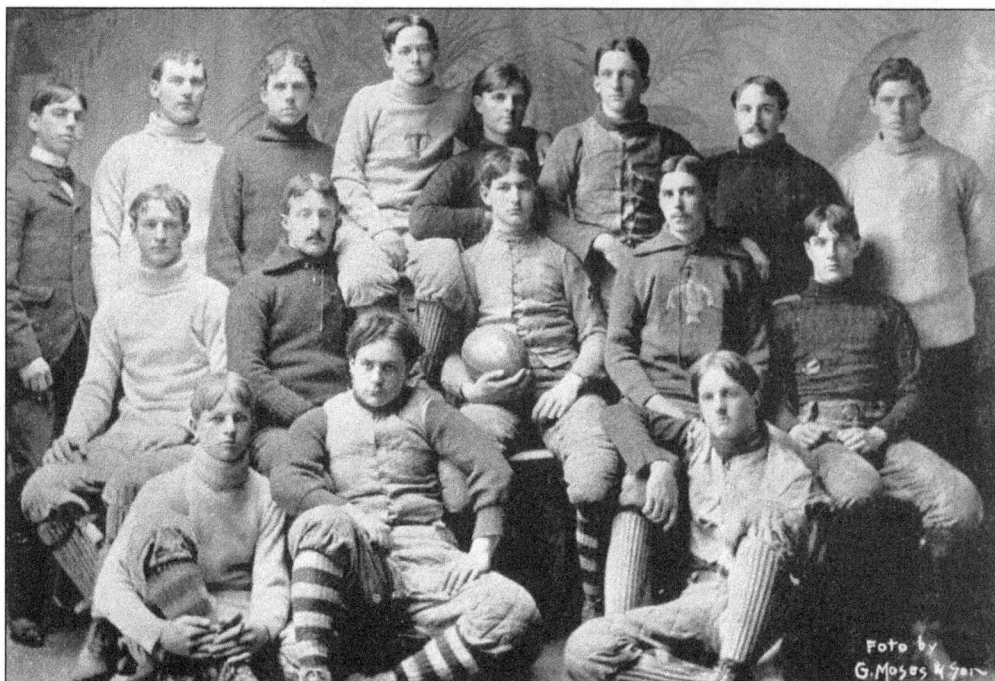

An athletic field was laid out in the back of campus in 1895, in the grassy area to the west of the workshops. A kite-shaped quarter-mile track was installed with a football field and baseball diamond nestled within it. Stands provided seating for about 3,000 spectators. The Tulane football team shown here hosted the University of Alabama as its first intercollegiate guest on November 17, 1895, winning its first home game 22-0. The stadium was relocated across Freret Street in 1910.

Tilton Hall, erected at the west end of Gibson Hall, was designed in the Richardsonian Romanesque style to match Gibson Hall. It was named for Frederick W. Tilton, husband of Caroline Tilton, who donated $50,000 for a library in her husband's memory. After the library grew too large for the building and was moved into the Howard-Tilton Memorial Library building on Freret Street in 1941, the Law School moved into Tilton Hall.

The School of Architecture got its beginnings in 1907 as a department within the College of Technology under the instruction of William Woodward and Samuel Labouisse. Nathaniel Cortlandt Curtis joined the faculty a few years later, and the program was firmly entrenched within Stanley Thomas Hall by 1911. A fourth floor was added to the building in 1929 under the direction of J. Herndon Thomson, professor of architecture.

This Richardson Memorial building was erected in 1908 to house the laboratories and classrooms for the first- and second-year medical students. Ivy from the old Richardson Memorial was planted here, perpetuating the Ivy Day ceremony, which is part of the School of Medicine's graduation ceremony. Medical students continued to use this building until 1963, when all coursework moved downtown to the medical center and this building was renovated and converted to the home of the School of Architecture.

BULLETIN OF THE
TULANE UNIVERSITY OF LOUISIANA

THE COLLEGE OF MEDICINE
SCHOOL OF HYGIENE AND
TROPICAL MEDICINE
INCLUDING PREVENTIVE MEDICINE

Situated in an area once besieged by repeated epidemics of yellow fever and malaria, New Orleans is a natural laboratory for teaching and learning about tropical diseases. In 1912, businessman Samuel Zemurray of the United Fruit Company contributed $25,000 to the university to establish the School of Hygiene and Tropical Medicine. It was the first such school in the United States.

One of the most enduring traditions at Newcomb was the May Day celebration, an annual festival that began in 1897. Each year, the juniors honored seniors with a performance that included dancing around a Maypole, weaving ribbons. In 1914, the queen, Theodora Sumner, was given a crown and scepter of flowers by the juniors and a large bouquet by the sophomores; her six maids received baskets of sweet peas.

52

Despite a clamor as early as 1848 for a college of commerce at the university, the feat was not accomplished until 1914, when a group of 104 guarantors from the business community agreed to underwrite the new college's expenses for a three-year period and the College of Commerce and Business Administration was formed. These were the first candidates for the bachelor of business degree in 1916.

In order to finance a new stadium, a university fundraising plan called Realization Day was held on March 31, 1916. Newcomb and Tulane students were given a school holiday to work that day in the city, their wages to be contributed to the new stadium fund. Citywide support was overwhelming, and the campaign netted $24,000 in wages and pledges in just that one day. Work began on a new concrete grandstand in May 1916, and the 30-tier grandstand, complete with covered press box, was ready in time for the 1917 season. The new Tulane Stadium, still located on Freret Street, was dedicated on October 27, 1917.

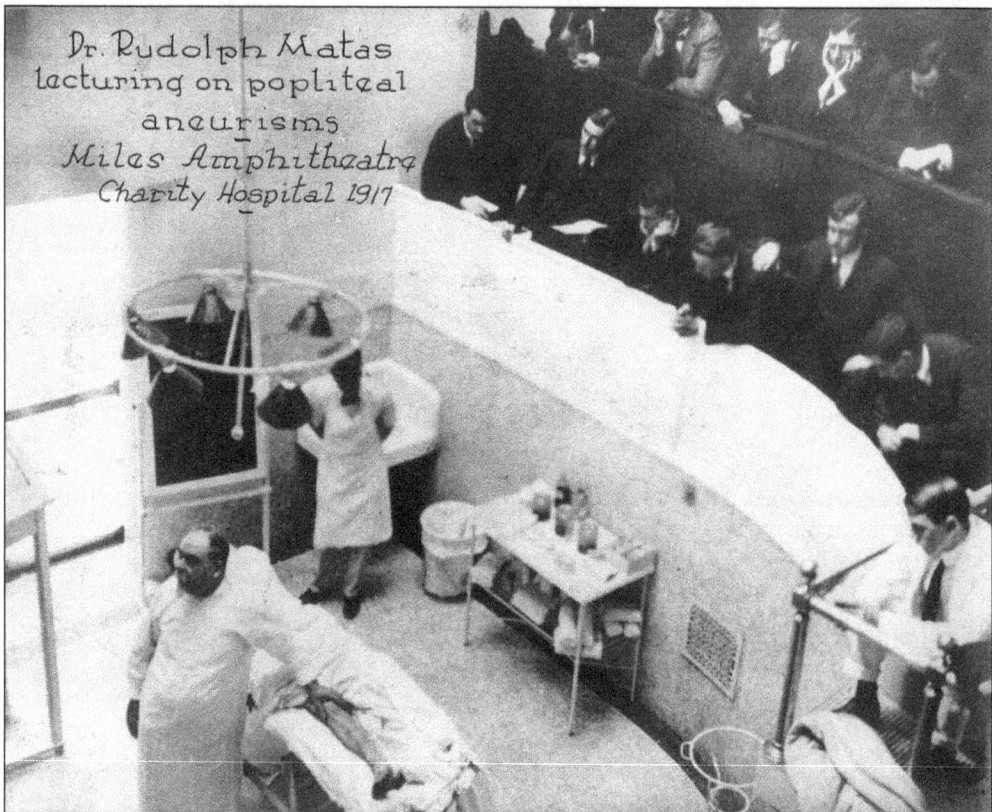

Dr. Rudolph Matas
lecturing on popliteal
aneurisms
Miles Amphitheatre
Charity Hospital 1917

Rudolph Matas (doctor of medicine, 1880) was one of the most accomplished medical professors and lecturers in the history of the university. In 50 years at Tulane, Dr. Matas gained distinction as a pioneer in vascular surgery, being the first to surgically repair aneurisms, to use spinal anesthesia, and to develop the intravenous drip technique. In 1937, the medical school library was named in his honor.

Having once again outgrown its campus, Newcomb College moved to a parcel of land adjoining the northwestern side of Tulane's campus in 1918. Newcomb's campus consisted of Newcomb Hall (pictured), the Art School, and the Josephine Louise House. All three buildings were constructed in the Italian Renaissance style by Joseph Gamble Rogers. Newcomb Hall housed the administrative offices and academic classrooms for the Newcomb students.

The Art School, situated on the north side of the quadrangle in front of Newcomb Hall, housed the Newcomb Pottery workshops and kilns, art classrooms, studios, and galleries. The oak trees in front of Newcomb quad today are offspring of original oaks from the Garden District campus. They were grown from acorns planted by Newcomb students in 1909 and were transplanted from the old campus when the Broadway campus was finally ready to be occupied.

The new Josephine Louise House was designed to hold 200 Newcomb students. In late September 1918, just as the students had moved in to begin the semester, the Spanish influenza epidemic struck. The dormitory was used as an infirmary where eventually 50 Newcomb students were put under quarantine. Per the mayor's orders, the quarantine lasted over a month; during that time, the students were not permitted to leave the city.

Beginning in September 1918, the 1,200 men in the Student Army Training Corps (SATC) were housed and trained in 14 wooden barracks erected in the quad behind Gibson Hall, extending across Freret Street to behind the gymnasium. Camp Martin relocated here from the fairgrounds, where it had been previously established. Soon after it opened, the Spanish influenza epidemic struck, and the Tulane students, being under military law due to the SATC contract, were quarantined by the US Army for three weeks. Above, in a view that looks more like Europe than Louisiana, barracks are aligned along "Company Street," which leads from Freret Street past the dormitory (now Fortier Hall) towards the rear of the Physics building (now Hebert Hall). Below, many men could be fed at one seating in the mess hall.

SATC students were provided with everything they would need, including room, board, tuition, uniforms, and a small stipend. Coursework, including radio mechanics, above, and motor mechanics, below, was taught by academic faculty and military officers. Camp Martin was on active duty on campus for only three months before the Armistice signaled the end of the war and the camp was demobilized. Altogether, 75 percent of the Tulane faculty was involved in war training in some capacity, through education or training or in medical service overseas with the Tulane Unit, Base Hospital No. 24.

Under Rudolph Matas's direction, a 500-bed hospital known as the Tulane Unit, Base Hospital No. 24, was established during World War I. It was equipped by the New Orleans chapter of the American Red Cross and staffed by Tulane Medical School professors and students. Dr. Matas was deemed too essential to be deployed, so he remained in New Orleans when the unit departed for Limoges, France, in September 1917. The hospital served with distinction, returning in April 1919.

Newcomb students contributed to the war effort through first aid training and rolling bandages, but their most organized accomplishment was to raise money for the Newcomb Relief Unit, a group of eight students who left in December 1918 to participate in canteen service in France through the summer of 1919. From left to right are (seated) Edith Dupre, Caroline Richardson, and Anna Many; (standing) Edna Danziger, Celeste Eshleman, Marion Monroe, Mary Palfrey, and Nettie Barnwell.

The Rolling Green Wave

They rolled their own in the army;
   And the fair femmes roll 'em, too;
But they roll the other fellow—
   Down by the Hullabaloo.

Oh, roll 'em; roll 'em; roll 'em;
   Roll 'em, you Rolling Green Wave;
Give 'em what they came for—
   Give 'em a deep green grave.
Fight 'em; fight 'em; fight 'em;
   Fight 'em, old T. U.;
Oh, if they won't say you're master,
   Just roll 'em some more till they do.

Now Tech's got a Gold Tornado;
   And Alabama a Thin Red Line;
But we've got a Rolling Green Breaker
   That'll cover 'em every time.

Oh, break 'em; break 'em; break 'em;
   Break 'em, you Great Green Wave;
Break 'em; shake 'em; make 'em
   Lie down in the deep green grave.
Ram 'em; jam 'em; cram 'em;
   At 'em, old T. U.;
And if they don't say you're master,
   Just keep it up till they do.

The Tiger's got his stripes on,
And the War Skule thinks he's mean,
But the growls will cease, for the raging
      beast
Will drown in the Rolling Green.

—E. E. SPARLING.

The athletic team owes its nickname to Earl Sparling (bachelor of science, 1921), editor of the student newspaper. In the October 29, 1920, edition of the *Hullabaloo* (which he renamed from the *Tulane Weekly*), he published his football song, "The Rolling Green Wave." The mainstream press picked up the moniker, first using it on November 12, 1920. Five years later, Tulane officially adopted a fight song, "The Olive and Blue," and its chorus, "Roll, Green Wave," cemented the nickname in place.

Although they had been on separate campuses before 1918, Newcomb women had always been very supportive of the Tulane men. Rosa Hart became the nation's first female cheerleader, jumping and yelling alongside her Tulane counterparts at Tulane's football games from 1920 to 1921. She blazed the trail for Marian Draper, shown here cheering in front of Tulane freshmen wearing their beanies in 1924.

Newcomb's School of Music, whose facilities were scattered in three houses around the neighborhood since leaving the Garden District campus, hosted a Realization Day on March 28, 1924, to raise money to erect a new music building with an auditorium on its campus. As they had in 1916, students spent the day working in factories and shops, selling bananas, pralines, and toothbrushes, and doing hundreds of other small money-making tasks to help raise funds. Progress was slow; Dixon Hall was not dedicated until 1929. Leon Ryder Maxwell was the director of the Newcomb School of Music. Unfortunately, famed composer and pianist Giuseppe Ferrata never had a chance to teach in the new building; he passed away in 1928, after having given 19 years of instruction to Newcomb students.

The Department of Middle American Research (DMAR) was established in 1924 through an endowment by Samuel Zemurray. The DMAR, led by archaeologist Frans Blom, far left, set out on its first expedition into the jungles of Mesoamerica in 1925. Its findings were reported in *Tribes and Temples*, the first of many publications for the department, which is now known as the Middle American Research Institute. This photograph is from the 1927 field season.

The 1925 football team was spectacularly successful under coach Clark Shaughnessy, with quarterback Lester Lautenschlaeger directing the action and All-American Charles "Peggy" Flournoy, shown here, leading the nation in scoring with 128 points. The Greenies earned an invitation to the Rose Bowl, which the board of administrators declined, thinking that it would take the students away from their studies for too long. The team's success inspired the university to build a larger stadium.

On October 23, 1926, fifteen thousand fans turned out to watch the Green Wave host its first intercollegiate football game in the new Tulane Stadium; unfortunately, Tulane was beaten by Auburn, 2-0. Designed by Emile Weil, the 35,000-seat stadium was constructed as two curved sections, built of brick and concrete, flanking the sidelines. Its $300,000 price tag was funded through public subscription. By 1947, the stadium had been enlarged to hold 80,000.

The School of Social Work got its start in 1914, when Tulane's social science faculty offered classes at Kingsley House in support of the Southern School of Social Sciences and Public Services' training program. Tulane took on the role of running its own social work program in 1921, upgrading it to a degree-granting school in 1927. Under the 26-year leadership of Elizabeth Wisner, shown here, the school became highly regarded across the nation.

By the late 1920s, the old Hutchinson Memorial on Canal Street had grown outdated and too small. The university received a $1.25-million grant to build a new Hutchinson Memorial Medical Building immediately adjacent to Charity Hospital. Dedicated in 1930, the new medical school building contained 145,000 square feet of space for offices, classrooms, a library, an auditorium, laboratories, clinics, and examining rooms that simulated private practice conditions.

From 1929 to 1931, the Green Wave football team amassed a 28-1 regular season record, losing only the second game of the 1930 season to Northwestern. It finally received another bid to the Rose Bowl in 1931 and accepted this time, but lost to the University of Southern California 21-12. To this day, the Greenies have never matched the streak of 18 straight wins that they achieved behind the spectacular play of men such as Red Dawson, Preacher Roberts, Nollie Felts, and All-Americans Bill Banker, Jerry Dalrymple, and Don Zimmerman.

The success of the Green Wave football team in the early 1930s inspired the New Orleans Mid-Winter Sports Association to propose a postseason football game to be held annually on New Year's Day in Tulane Stadium: the Sugar Bowl. In the inaugural game, Monk Simons's heroics helped Tulane to triumph over Temple University by a score of 20-14. Tulane played again in 1940 but lost to Texas A&M 14-13.

Heading to Baton Rouge on the Illinois Central Railway, the Tulane University Band occupied the "Blue" train, the first railcar to leave for the big game against Louisiana State University on the morning of November 28, 1936. The football team came next on the "Green" train, leaving at 8:45 a.m., then faculty and other private coaches followed. Tulane lost miserably that day, cementing LSU's undefeated season and ensuring its repeat bid to the Sugar Bowl.

In 1938, Pres. Rufus Harris applied to establish a Naval Reserve Officer Training Corps (NROTC) unit at Tulane and, with the help of retired Vice Adm. Ernest L. Jahncke (bachelor of engineering, 1899), was selected. Tulane's was the eighth collegiate unit to be established. A full quota of 76 NROTC candidates enrolled the first year.

The Student Center stood between Alcée Fortier Hall and Freret Street, where the west end of Percival Stern Hall sits. It was built in 1940 with funds raised by the alumni association, and housed the offices of that group and of the student publications, as well as providing social spaces that included a game room, ballroom, and soda fountain. It was demolished in 1969 to make way for Stern Hall.

McAlister Auditorium, which contains the world's largest self-suspended concrete dome, was built in 1940 by local architects Favrot and Reed. The dome "breathes" to prevent cracking. It was erected through a bequest from Amelie McAlister Upshur as a memorial to her mother. The Art Deco building seats about 1,950, and has been used for concerts, convocations, town hall meetings, graduations, and award ceremonies.

The Cunningham Observatory, built next to McAlister Auditorium in 1941, housed the Calver telescope that had been used by noted astronomer William H. Pickering in his observatory in Jamaica. The building was torn down in 2001 to make room for Goldring-Woldenberg Hall II, and a new observatory was built on the roof of Jones Hall.

In 1938, a decision was made to consolidate the undergraduate Newcomb and Tilton Libraries. Importantly, the city's Howard Library would join them, bringing an annual income that would enable the university to erect a new building to house the confederated collection. The new Howard-Tilton Memorial Library, specially equipped with air-conditioning and a seven-level book stack in the center of the three-story building, opened in 1941 on Freret Street.

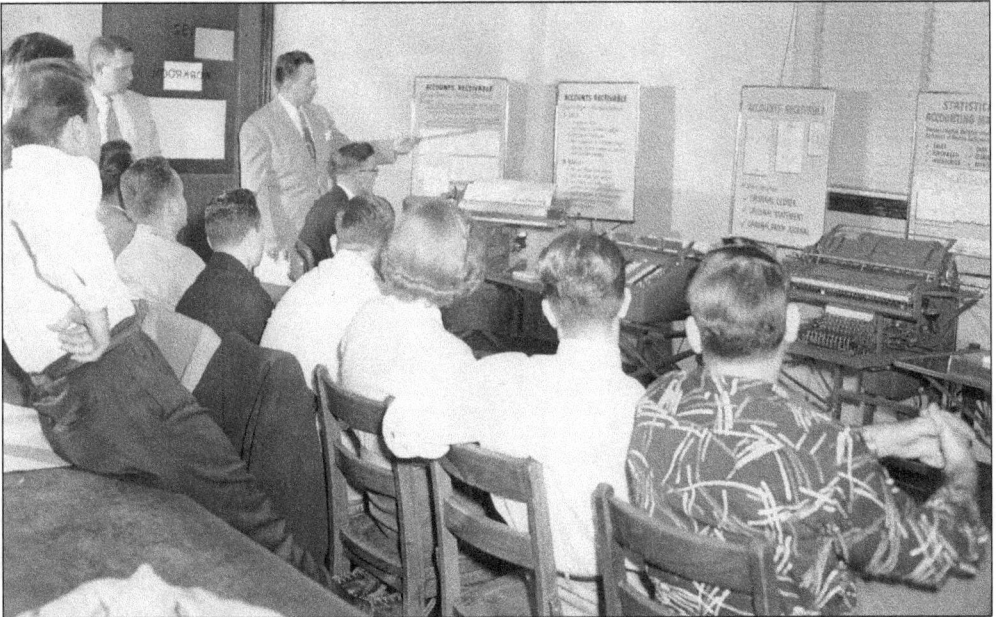

The Tulane College of Commerce and Business Administration offered night courses in business that admitted both men and women. Classes were held in Gibson Hall from 8:00 to 9:45 p.m. one night a week to enable students to take up to four courses during a semester. Coursework was offered in accounting, advertising, commercial law, management of employees, salesmanship, and Spanish business correspondence.

The university's long-standing commitment to offering educational opportunities at night and on weekends to adults with full-time careers was formalized with the creation of University College in 1942. It combined the former Division for Teachers and the College of Commerce and Business Administration's Night Division, offering 75 degrees at an affordable $7.50 per credit hour. Thirty-one baccalaureate degrees were awarded the first year.

At the request of the US surgeon general in 1942, the medical school reactivated its mobile medical unit, the 24th General Hospital, under the command of alumnus Col. Walter C. Royals (doctor of medicine, 1917). The Tulane Unit, comprised of 30 medical graduates and 10 faculty members from the university, served stateside at Fort Benning, in Tunisia, and in three cities in Italy, including at Army headquarters near Florence, between 1942 and 1945, earning the Fifth Army Plaque and Clasp for meritorious service. (RMLHS.)

High-flying Idamay Hayden soars over (from left to right) Al Robinson, Jimmy McConnell, Betty Blain Lyle, and Bob Murray in a photograph shot for the Cam-Pix section of the *Greenie*, the Tulane football magazine, on October 23, 1943. The men were Navy V-12 students who doubled as cheerleaders, and the women were Newcomb students who were cheerleaders and also members of the same sorority, Delta Zeta, as well as spirit club and dance club members.

The accelerated Navy college training program, Navy V-12, brought over 1,100 students to campus from 1943 to 1945, offering coursework in engineering, the sciences, medicine, and business administration. The gymnasium, now known as Devlin Fieldhouse, was converted into a dormitory to house the Navy students, and other buildings were repurposed to accommodate the influx as well. Pictured is the first inspection of the V-12 unit in July 1943.

By the time that World War II had concluded, 4,000 alumni and 150 faculty and staff had served in some capacity. These 121 members of the Tulane community paid the ultimate price and were honored with a plaque that hung in the Student Center, where the Kendall Cram Room was also named in honor of the fallen former director of student activities and alumni activities.

Three

MODERNIZATION OF THE UNIVERSITY 1945–2005

After World War II, finances were lean, so the university embarked upon a long-range fundraising program called the Tulane Educational Advancement Program. This ultimately led to the establishment of the Development Division, which created revenue through solicitation of annual gifts, individual pledges, estate planning, and alumni giving.

Academically, Tulane began the transition from local college to research university, strengthening both undergraduate and graduate programs, locally and internationally, and the number of faculty and students increased dramatically. In order to accommodate the population explosion, over a 15-year period, the university built nine dormitories, a university center, a field house, a swimming pool, a health services building, two food service buildings, and a power plant.

The 1950s and 1960s saw many changes in the nature of the student body. The opening of the University of New Orleans in 1956 offered another local option for higher education for residents, thus diverting some of the homegrown customers away from Tulane. The university responded by recruiting students from farther and farther away, which changed the identity of Tulane from a commuter college to a residential college.

A significant change in student body composition was brought by desegregation in January 1963. Although prospective African American students, the Graduate School faculty, and the president had all tried since the early 1950s to convince the board to allow integration, it took a lawsuit that ran from April 1961 to December 1962 for the matter to be settled.

During that time, some of the student body found unity through activism, participating in interracial cafeteria sit-ins both on-campus and off-campus. Student activism later focused on the Vietnam War. Protests, an interrupted ROTC drill, a fire-bombed building, and the occupation of the University Center were examples of campus disturbances during 1969 and 1970.

In 1975, Pres. Gerald Ford announced the end of American involvement in the Vietnam War while giving a speech in the basketball gymnasium. The final quarter-century brought rapidly evolving technological improvements in an environment of escalating costs, milestone anniversaries, undergraduate school identity conflicts, athletic struggles and achievements, and anxious anticipation for the new millennium.

Tulane Stadium had been expanded several times at the behest and the expense of the organization that sponsored the annual Sugar Bowl competition. Consequently, Tulane benefitted from a stadium that would hold 80,000 fans by midcentury. This 1939 photograph shows the stadium when it could hold about 72,000 spectators after completion of the upper-deck segments.

On the fifth day of a citywide garbage strike, New Orleans mayor deLesseps S. Morrison asked for volunteers on October 28, 1946, to help collect the weekend's accumulation of garbage. Answering the call were, from left to right, law students Dolan Tipping, Bowman Goetzman, Jack Bremermann, and Frank Moise, all ex-Marines; a contingent of fraternity members and other students also volunteered. Pres. Rufus Harris excused all volunteers from classes.

A group of four physics graduate students (John Tallant, Cameron Byrne, Hal Becker, and Fred Schmidt) built the first amateur, noncommercial television station in the South and transmitted a two-hour broadcast to a receiver in the president's office on August 11, 1948. The signal was sent from the same physics building where, 50 years earlier, the first radio signal ever sent in the South was broadcast by two Tulane students.

After lackluster enrollment numbers in the early 20th century, interest in public health and tropical medicine coursework began to gain traction. In 1945, the William Henderson Chair of Tropical Medicine was established, preceding the formation of the Department of Tropical Medicine and Public Health by two years. Faculty and enrollment expanded rapidly, and in 1949, coursework leading to a doctorate in public health was offered.

A Newcomb swimming club that began in 1938 morphed into the Barracuda Club by 1949. Specializing in synchronized aquatics, Newcomb students presented an annual water ballet each spring. By accumulating points based on participation and enthusiasm in sports such as swimming, badminton, bowling, archery, tennis, ping pong, and basketball, a student could earn the most coveted athletic award for women, a Newcomb blanket.

Although various student groups had been presenting talent shows since each college's establishment, these coalesced into an annual production called Campus Nite, written and performed by Tulane and Newcomb students and staff, by 1949. In this photograph from a 1950s production, *"Dig Your Grave"—with Sam Shovel*, director and lyricist Wynne Pearce sings in his role as Crudest Dude, while lead actor Ed Nelson, as detective Sam Shovel, listens.

After a spirited pep rally (and tiger-napping) and shirt-tail parade in downtown New Orleans in which cheerleaders and members of TUSK, the Tulane University Spirit Klub, rode on an Army ROTC Duck vehicle, Tulane and Louisiana State University played the 1950 homecoming game in front of 72,000 fans. They battled to a 14-14 tie, which meant that each team got to keep the Rag, symbol of the longtime competitive spirit between the two rivals, for six months. Below, No. 66 Alan Hover, LSU right tackle, and Dabney Ewin, president of the Tulane Student Council, shake hands, while No. 52 Joe Reid, LSU center, and No. 60 Dennis Doyle, Tulane right guard, look on.

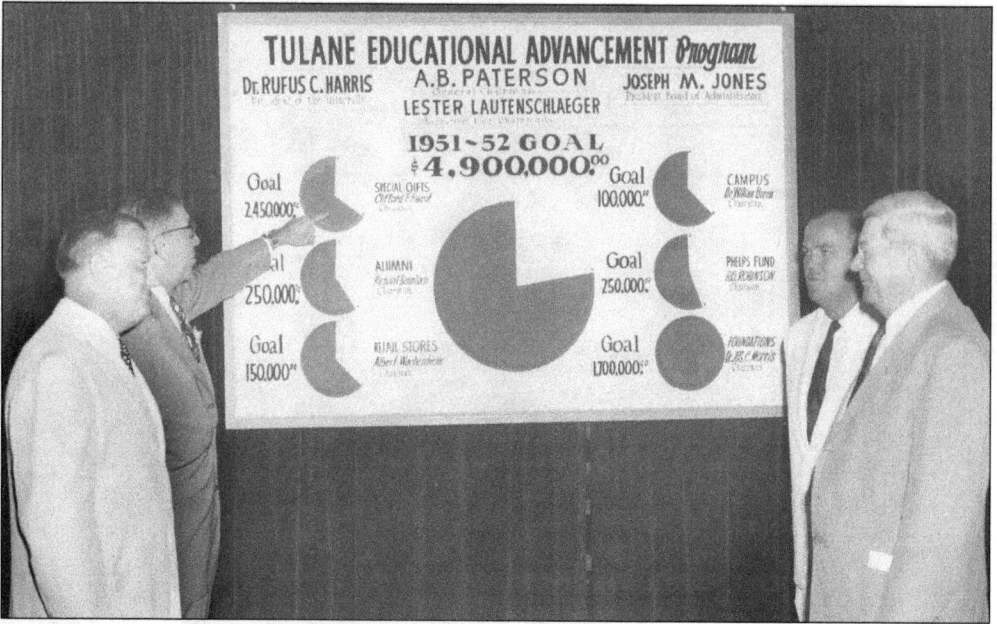

After raising over $2 million in the first phase of a long-range plan to increase the university's endowment in 1951, from left to right, Pres. Rufus Harris and board members Clifford Favrot, Joseph M. Jones, and A.B. Paterson review the goal of the second phase, which would result in a $4.9-million increase in the general endowment. The university's fundraising success would be augmented by matching grants from the General Education Board of New York.

The theme of the annual Beaux Arts Ball in 1952 was *Les Jours des Fêtes*, or Holidays. Sponsored by the Women's Auxiliary of the American Institute of Architects, the ball's proceeds funded a summer travel scholarship for an architecture student. This image shows costumes celebrating the holidays of St. Patrick's Day, Christmas, and Valentine's Day following an intriguing entry into the ball.

After a preliminary elimination round, five sororities made it to the finals of the Sorority Skit Nite competition in 1953. Alpha Epsilon Phi won bragging rights for best skit with "Twenty-Two Skidoo," their production that celebrated the days of bathroom gin, flappers, the Charleston, and historic Tulane victories over rival Louisiana State University. Chi Omega took second place.

The Fraternity Skit Nite was held two months later, following a similar format of an early elimination round and a final presentation. This image shows Zeta Beta Tau's entry of "Versus Vice," in which three prim Newcomb chaperones visit the ideal Tulane campus in outer space and return to extol the virtues of the younger set at Newcomb. Unfortunately, the newspapers do not record which fraternity won the competition.

Within a six-year period, the university built five new dormitories to house the explosion of new residential students. Around this quad, clockwise from left, are Phelps (1954, for men), Zemurray (1949, for male athletes), Paterson (1951, for men), and Irby Houses (1954, for men). Johnston House, for graduate women, was also built nearby in 1955; it was replaced by the Mayer Residences in 1997.

One of the most memorable events for students from the mid-1950s was the unexpected panty raid that happened on the night of October 18, 1954. That evening, two Newcomb students looking for "George" at Phelps House unintentionally incited a crowd of 500 Tulane students into staging a panty raid on the Newcomb campus. Ultimately, city police were called in to quell the "riot," and four Tulane students were arrested for disturbing the peace.

The first full Newcomb Junior Year Abroad class, on their way to Paris on the *Ile de France* in 1955, gathered in Rockefeller Plaza. They are, from left to right, (first row) Barbara Evans, Frances Farrell, Genevieve Wilson, Lida Mae Smith, Martha Ann Guy, Madelene Stone, Vivian Burch, Helen Allen, Margaret Celli, and Johanna Hammell; (second row) Sarah Lee Colquitt, Marilyn Arnoult, Mignon Faget, Nancy Nichols, Ana Maria Lamar, Mabel Anderson, Gail Jean Price, Amanda Brown, Eva Loridans, Blanche MacFadyen, Ellen Wright, and Jennifer Mann.

The Caroline Richardson Building was erected in 1958 to provide a single dining hall for all Newcomb students living on campus. Named for an alumna (bachelor of arts, 1895; master of arts, 1905) and English professor, the building was repurposed in 1975 as the home of the Newcomb Women's Center, currently known as the Newcomb College Center for Research on Women. The Newcomb Archives and Vorhoff Library are located here.

Under coach Emmett Paré, Tulane tennis teams racked up 18 Southeastern Conference championships, including a run of nine straight from 1951 to 1959; in 1959, Tulane won the NCAA team national championship as well. Paré also coached four Tulanians who became national intercollegiate singles champions: Ernie Sutter (1936–1937), Jack Tuero (1949), Hamilton Richardson (1953–1954, shown here with "Coach"), and José "Pepe" Aguero (1955). Paré also coached women's tennis star Linda Tuero.

The first computer arrived on campus in May 1958 as a result of the School of Business Administration's focus on quantitative analysis and problem-solving skills that could be honed through computerized management games. Dr. James W. Sweeney was director of the computer center in the Norman Mayer Building, which held a suite of IBM machines: a 650 computer, an 026 punch-card machine, an 077 collator, a 402 accounting machine, and a 514 reproducing punch machine.

Rosen House was built in 1959 as a residence hall for married students and as temporary housing for new faculty. It was later opened to unmarried graduate students, international students, and student athletes. Situated on South Claiborne Avenue, it marked the northern border of campus. After taking on several feet of water during Katrina, it was demolished and replaced with a surface parking lot.

The University Center, on McAlister Drive, opened in 1959 as the social center of campus. It held a student food services area, faculty dining room, bookstore, student lounges, the Monk Simons Swimming Pool, the Kendall Cram Room, offices for student media groups like the *Hullabaloo* and *Jambalaya* staffs and the WTUL radio station, a barbershop, a bowling alley, a game room, and the ever-popular Rathskellar, where the Tulanians and other musical acts performed.

Dr. Joseph E. Gordon came to Tulane in 1954 as the assistant dean of University College and an instructor in mathematics, but he hopscotched his way upward through different administrative positions until 1964, when he became dean of the College of Arts and Sciences. His steady leadership in that position stretched for 20 years, the longest tenure in Tulane's history. He continued as emeritus dean until 1996.

Standing on one of the balconies of the 12-story Monroe Hall afforded students a great view of the middle portion of campus. Built in 1963, Monroe towered over its seven- and four-story, L-shaped neighboring dormitory, Sharp Hall, which had been constructed three years earlier. Butler House, the eight-story honors student dormitory that stood on Willow Street near the stadium, was also built in 1963.

Tulane received $2.5 million in funding from the National Institutes of Health in 1962 to establish the Delta Regional Primate Research Center in Covington, Louisiana. The compound consisted of five buildings on 500 acres that housed laboratories, administrative functions, and animal cages. Dr. Arthur J. Riopelle was its inaugural director. Now one of eight centers in the National Primate Research Center Program, its primary area of research is infectious diseases.

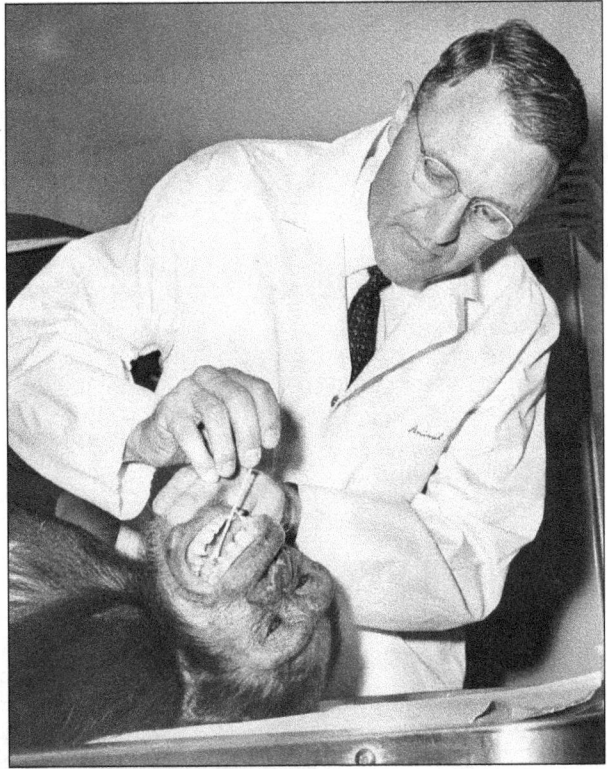

When he was still in medical school at Tulane in 1931, studying under Alton Ochsner, Michael E. DeBakey invented a roller pump that became an essential component of the heart-lung machine that enabled open-heart surgery 20 years later. Other innovations include Dacron artificial arteries in 1953, the first successful coronary artery bypass in 1964, and some of the first heart transplants. Shown here with Rudolph Matas in 1954, DeBakey, right, was on the Tulane faculty in the Department of Surgery from 1937 to 1948.

In April 1961, Tulane's board released a statement that it would permit qualified students regardless of race or color if it were legally permissible. After two well-qualified African American students were denied enrollment in the School of Social Work, a lawsuit was filed on behalf of the women. The final ruling in December 1962, confirming that Tulane was a private institution that could voluntarily admit students of color, led to the board's immediate implementation of the April 1961 policy, beginning with the enrollment of 11 African American students in January 1963. These were primarily graduate and evening students, including Gloria Adams, who is shown at far left registering in the Graduate School. Reynold T. Décou (bachelor of science, 1967; bachelor of arts, 1979), shown below in a geology class in 1966, enrolled in the College of Arts and Sciences in fall 1963. Décou and Newcomb transfer student Deidre Ann Dumas (bachelor of science, 1966; master of science, 1969) blazed the trail as the only traditional undergraduates to complete the 1963–1964 academic year. (Left, UPI.)

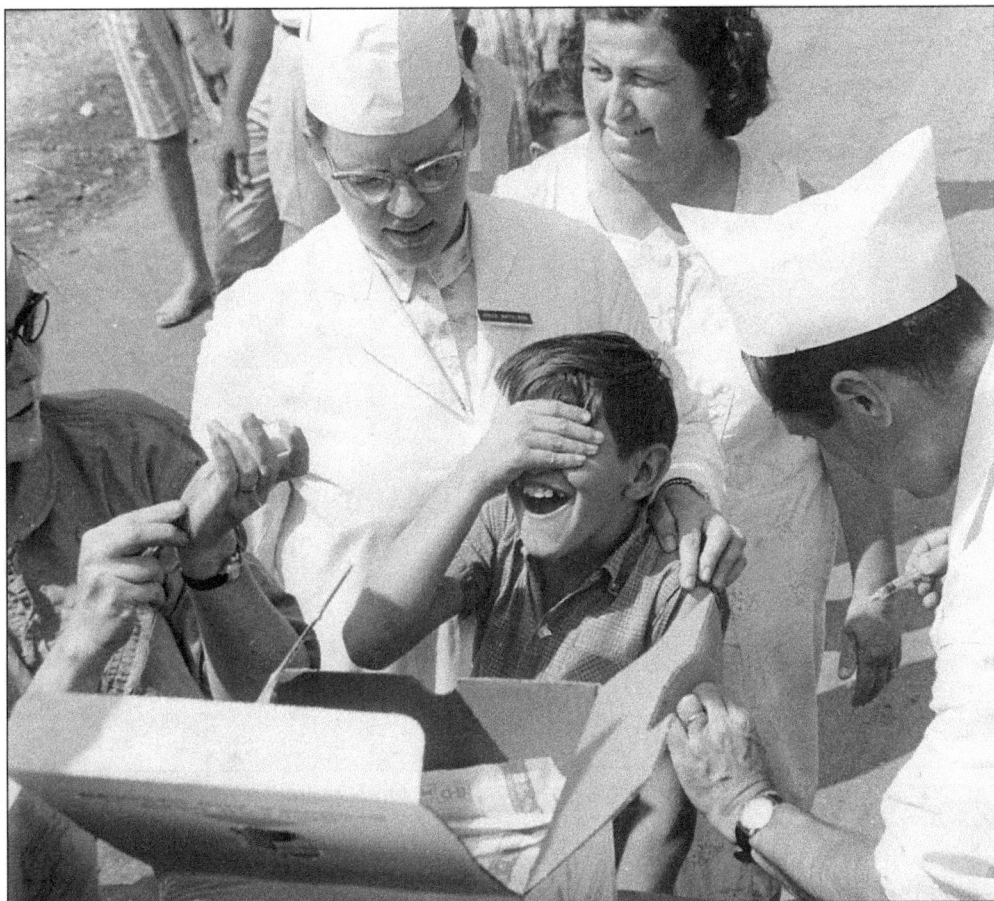

Hurricane Betsy struck New Orleans on September 9, 1965. Emergency preparations began on September 5, and by September 8, everyone was hunkered down and ready to wait out the storm. On September 9, winds gusted to 150 miles per hour by 8:00 p.m., and the telephones and lights went out. A top wind of 160 miles per hour hit at midnight, then the storm eased. Power was out for three days; telephones were out for 10 days. To help with disaster relief in the city, Tulane medical students were called on to assist in providing immunizations and to provide general medical care for thousands of evacuees housed at an army base in the week after the storm. Damage to campus was estimated at $300,000.

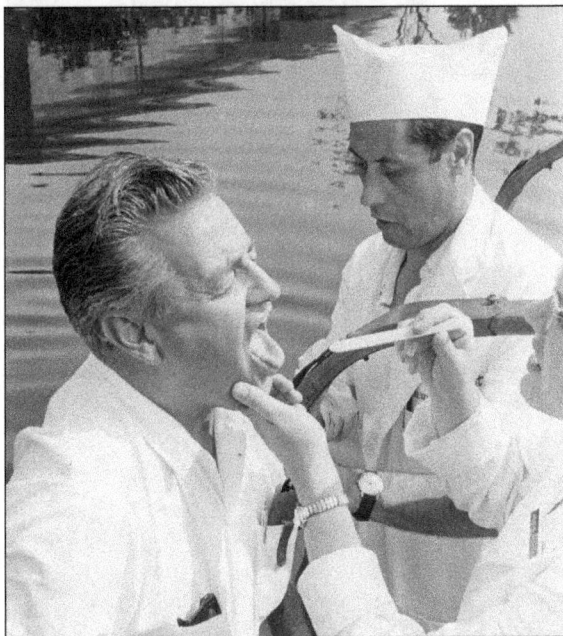

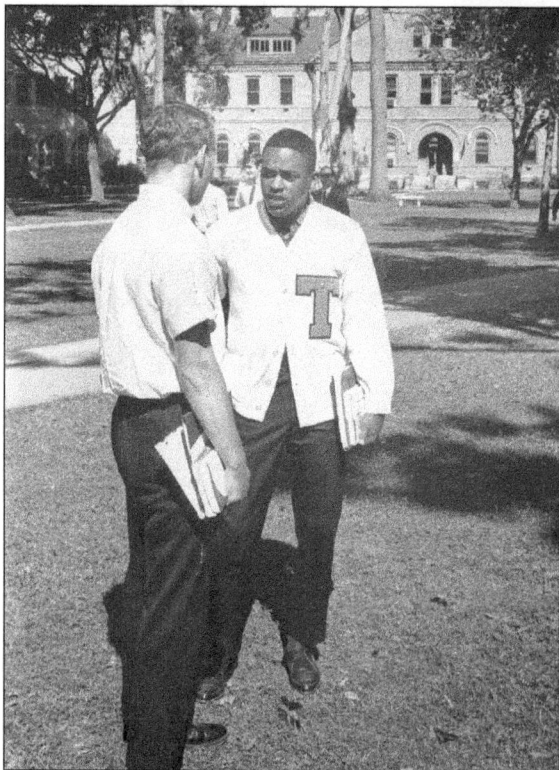

On September 17, 1967, the New Orleans Saints played their first home football game in front of 80,879 fans in Tulane Stadium. The Saints played here for eight seasons, amassing a 23-32-1 record. The NFL also loved Tulane Stadium—it held three of the first nine Super Bowls here (1970, 1972, 1975). The stadium was the site of the 63-yard Tom Dempsey field goal that set a kicking record that stood for 43 years.

Stephen Martin entered Tulane in the fall of 1964. When he took the field for the Green Wave baseball team in 1966, he became the first African American varsity athlete to compete in the Southeastern Conference. A Rockefeller Scholar, he earned a bachelor of arts in Latin in 1968 and master's in business administration in 1973. He became the vice president for finance at Tuskegee University in 2011.

When the library outgrew its building, a new edifice was constructed directly across Newcomb Boulevard. The books were shifted to the new building via a plastic-enclosed wooden ramp and 11,271 book truck trips. The modern building opened in 1968 with four floors of browsable stacks and a student lounge and snack area in the basement. The new Howard-Tilton Library was designed to carry two additional floors, an asset that came into play after Hurricane Katrina struck almost 40 years later.

CACTUS, the Community Action Council of Tulane University Students, was officially established in the spring of 1968. With administrative support, students' previous involvement in service projects quadrupled, enabling more than 60 students to participate in projects such as Project Opportunity, in which students worked with budding scholars at Priestly Junior High School, and DARE, a recreational program.

Anti-war sentiment simmered on campus throughout the late 1960s but peaked in late April 1969, when protesting students and faculty member Edward Dubinsky interrupted several ROTC drills on the University Center quad. On April 29, a group of about 50 conducted a sit-in, despite being warned to move off the field by Col. Robert Scruton, director of university security; several of the students and Dubinsky were forcibly removed, some dragged from the field and arrested. A week later at the ROTC awards ceremony in McAlister Auditorium, the same protestors filled the upstairs balcony and disrupted the event. As a result, 21 students received sanctions for their actions, and Dubinsky's faculty appointment was terminated on the grounds of willfully disrupting regularly scheduled classes and academic activities.

Following a speech by "Chicago Seven" radical Rennie Davis on April 7, 1970, a group of students, accompanied by Davis, marched on Pres. Herbert Longenecker's house. He wasn't at home, so the group waited and discussed types of protest actions. Hours later, an Air Force barracks on campus was firebombed. Although several Molotov cocktails were found inside, no one was ever accused of having started the blaze.

The Tulane Hullabaloo

Vol. LXX No. 21   NEW ORLEANS, LOUISIANA, APRIL 10, 1970   Tel. 865-7711, Ext. 349

Five Hundred Students 'Liberate' University Center; Strike Of All Classes Planned For Noon Today

LIBERATION: The Free Speech Rally held Wednesday night in the University Center rapidly developed into a night long occupation by students.

(Photo by Buddy Brimberg)

A Summary Of The Week

TUESDAY, APRIL 7

Rennie Davis, a member of the "Chicago Seven," scheduled to speak in McAlister Auditorium at 4 p.m., refused to address the audience composed entirely of bearers of University identification cards. A crowd of non-affiliates was allowed to enter at 4:20, and Davis' speech

Coalition of Senate Candidates Formed

(Editor's Note: The following story was compiled from the notes of reporters Mike Simpson, Rick Streiffer, Ray Manning, Frank Coyne, and Kevin Allain. It was organized by Paul Baxter and Margaret Blain.)

A debate between two rival slates of candidates for Student Senate officers initiated a series of events which were climaxed late Thursday night with a decision by a meeting of some 500 students to begin a strike of classes at noon today.

The students who "occupied" part of the "liberated" University Center building continuously from Wednesday night designated themselves the Tulane Liberation Front (TLF). They indicated that they would make policy decisions for the student body in place of the traditional student government bodies.

The movement centered its program around a list of ten "demands" or "objectives." These included:

1) Self-rule for the faculty.
2) Student evaluation of the faculty.
3) Elimination of arbitrary social rules.
4) Creation of a viable atmosphere for blacks on the campus, as defined by the blacks themselves.
5) Implementation of a student bill of rights, to be made by students and faculty together and to be legally binding on the Administration.
6) Abolition of all ROTC courses, except those taught by regular academic personnel.
7) Invitation to the nine former students dismissed last year after anti-ROTC demonstrations to be reinstated in the University.
8) Reinstatement of Dr. Edward Dubinsky, former associate professor of mathematics, who was also dismissed after the demonstrations.
9) An end of censorship over campus speakers and publications.
10) Amnesty for all women students involved in dorm rules violations for staying in the U.C. overnight.

The most dramatic moments of TLF's first full day of existence Thursday came during an extended afternoon confrontation with President

Bored, Trout Form Coalition

Herbert E. Longenecker and several members of the Board of Administrators.

Questioned at length by a largely hostile crowd of students and faculty, Board members defended their firing of Dubinsky as proper and necessary, and affirmed that they would not reverse the decision under any circumstances.

Continued dissatisfaction with the president's and Board members' statements culminated in a declaration by graduate student David Kramer, a leader of TLF and moderator of the stormy session, that the University was "closed down."

Formally Ratified

This move was more formally ratified last night during a meeting of some 500 students in the U.C. Rejecting, after lengthy and heated debate, calls for a strike at 8 a.m. today, the LTF gathering voted to boycott classes starting at noon. Teachers of morning classes would be urged to call them off or to use them for discussion of the issues of the student revolt.

Meanwhile, committees of five students and five faculty members intended to try to meet Friday morning with members of the 42-member group of prominent

Inspired by the Davis speech, a group of opposing candidates formed the Tulane Liberation Front (TLF) to occupy the University Center. Renaming it the Student Union and threatening to boycott classes, they created a series of nine demands that they presented to Pres. Longenecker. None of the items were granted as written, and the six-day occupation ended peacefully when the student senate failed to support the TLF.

On May 5, 1970, Rick Madden spoke during an afternoon protest against the invasion of Cambodia and the killing of four students at Kent State University. Alongside mock graves that had been dug on the University Center quad, Nixon was burned in effigy. This demonstration was followed by an altercation at the Newcomb flagpole in which students wrestled over lowering the flag to half-staff in honor of their fallen collegiate colleagues.

Stern Hall is named for alumnus Percival Stern (bachelor of engineering, 1899), who pledged $3 million for this science building to be built. Made of reinforced concrete with walls of precast concrete, it is perhaps most well-known for its unique facade, which is reputed to represent an old-fashioned computer punch-card that would be read as "Roll Wave—Beat LSU" when fed into a computer.

On the evening of April 23, 1975, Pres. Gerald R. Ford made this stunning announcement in Tulane's basketball gymnasium to a crowd of 5,300 students and invited guests: "Today, America can again regain the sense of pride that existed before Vietnam. But it cannot be achieved by refighting a war that is finished—as far as America is concerned." For Americans, the Vietnam war had ended.

Tulane debuted three women's intercollegiate athletic teams in the 1975–1976 academic year: volleyball, basketball, and tennis. The volleyball team had a very successful season, posting a 20-10 record, winning the Association for Intercollegiate Athletics for Women state title, and advancing to the regional championships. The team was, from left to right, (first row) Gina Ello, Sara Speer, Kim Shaw, Becky Dalby, and Carol Graham; (second row) Susan Browne, Susan Folse, Betsy Wilkinson, Cindy Demarest, Sandy Paternostro, and coach Kay Metcalf.

With parts of the Tulane Stadium falling into disrepair, the board voted in November 1973 to move Tulane football games to the Superdome when it opened in 1975. Eighty percent of the students disapproved of the decision, mostly due to logistics and more restrictive alcohol regulations. Consequently, student attendance at games was low, especially in the later years. The 'Dome was the home field for the Green Wave for almost 40 years.

Groundbreaking for the 300-bed hospital and ambulatory care teaching facility, the center point of the Tulane University Medical Center located across the street from Hutchinson Memorial Medical Building, took place in 1973, with the building's dedication coming three years later. The $44.5-million complex allowed relocation of clinical facilities to a centralized location.

With parts of the stadium condemned and demolition set to begin on November 19, 1979, a "Farewell to Tulane Stadium" was scheduled for the evening of November 18. Every football player, cheerleader, and homecoming queen since 1920 was invited back for the event. Sugar Bowl–winning teams and Saints players were also invited. Tickets were sold for the gala; about 15,000 spectators attended. The program featured the strings and tympani from the New Orleans Symphony, Southern University Marching Band, Alvin Alcorn's Imperial Marching Band, the Feld Ballet Company of New York, the Tulane Pep Band, and the Tulanians musical group. An illustrated history of the 81,000-seat stadium was presented. Demolition began the following day and finished in 1980. Steel from the stadium, once the largest steel-structure stadium in the world, was repurposed into new construction at a motor speedway in another state.

Tulane is proud to claim two Nobel laureates among its past faculty. Dr. Andrew V. Schally, shown at far left being given an honorary doctor of medicine degree from Pres. Sheldon Hackney in 1978, received his Nobel Prize for Physiology and Medicine on December 10, 1977, for his pioneering efforts in endocrine research. Dr. Louis J. Ignarro, a professor of pharmacology at Tulane from 1973 to 1985, was awarded his Nobel Prize in 1986 based on his discoveries concerning nitric oxide as a signaling molecule in the cardiovascular system. Dr. Ignarro, below, donated a replica of his prize to the Rudolph Matas Library of the Health Sciences in 2002. (Below, RMLHS.)

Designed to unite visually the Tulane and Newcomb campuses by combining Richardsonian elements of front campus with the forms and red brick of Newcomb's campus, Goldring-Woldenberg Hall I was dedicated in 1986. It is the home of the A.B. Freeman School of Business. Goldring-Woldenberg Hall II, which houses graduate and executive programs and the Trading Center, opened in 2003.

Tulane's 150th birthday was celebrated during SesquiCelebration Week, September 16–23, 1984. Many of the university's 75,000 alumni were invited back to participate in the special exhibits, seminars, open houses, and tours and to attend the sesquicentennial convocation and a birthday party on the University Center quad afterward. Heavy rain drove the birthday party inside, where Pres. Eamon Kelly sliced the cake.

The Daisy Chain, one of Newcomb's oldest traditions, dates back to 1909. The chain of over 1,000 daisies was assembled by members of the junior class on the eve or early morning of commencement, then carried in procession to form an aisle through which the seniors and faculty pass. The tradition is continued in Newcomb College Institute's Under the Oaks ceremony. In this 1986 photograph, Dr. Karlem "Ducky" Riess, in his role as university marshal, stands ready to lead the faculty in procession following the Daisy Chain.

At this press conference, held on March 28, 1985, athletic director Hindman Wall (front) and basketball coach Ned Fowler discussed point-shaving allegations against members of the men's basketball team. That, along with illegal payments to a player by Coach Fowler, led Pres. Eamon Kelly to discontinue the basketball program on April 4, 1985. Both Wall and Fowler resigned within the week. Basketball was reinstated for the 1989 season.

The student-run Direction lecture series began in 1968 as a part of Tulane University Campus Programming, designed to bring renowned speakers to campus each spring to address topical themes. Covering the realms of politics, public service, arts and entertainment, journalism, activism, and education, notable speakers have included Ronald Reagan, Gerald Ford, George H. W. Bush (all before they were elected president), Andrew Young, Hunter S. Thompson, Ralph Nader, Jesse Jackson, Art Buchwald, Wendell Pierce, Robin Tyler, Allen Ginsberg, Malcolm Forbes, and alumnus Howard K. Smith (bachelor of arts, 1936), shown at right acting as moderator in 1979. Below, former presidents Jimmy Carter and Gerald Ford appeared on stage in 1985, moderated by alumnus William B. "Bill" Monroe Jr. (bachelor of arts, 1942) and introduced by Direction '85 chairman David Horrigan.

Newcomb kicked off a yearlong celebration in October 1986 with ceremonies in Dixon Hall honoring 15 recipients of the Newcomb Centennial Award, given to outstanding alumnae who embodied the spirit of Newcomb. Throughout the year, symposia, an exhibit of Newcomb pottery, and a half-hour television show commemorating Newcomb's 100th birthday were presented. The year culminated with the burying of a time capsule in Centennial Park, next to Newcomb gymnasium, shown here.

Over the protests of many alumnae, who feared that Newcomb's unique identity would be lost, the faculties of Newcomb College and Tulane's College of Arts and Sciences were merged in 1987. After the merger, each college still retained its own dean, its degree-granting status, and its students' self-governance. To ensure that Newcomb's identity was not weakened, the Newcomb Foundation was formed and initially funded by the board for the benefit of Newcomb College and its students. (NAVL.)

The Lindy Claiborne Boggs Center for Energy and Biotechnology was dedicated in March 1988, virtually doubling the space available to the School of Engineering. Named for treasured Newcomb alumna Corinne "Lindy" Claiborne Boggs (bachelor of arts, 1935), the 90,000-square-foot, energy-efficient building featured the Coordinated Research Instrumentation Facility and a multitude of laboratories for work in chemical, biomechanical, and environmental engineering.

The Reily Student Recreation Center opened in 1989 to serve the recreational needs of the university by providing facilities for intramural sports, weight training, exercise, and innovative fitness programs. Students voted to fund the center through paying an enhanced activity fee. It quickly became one of the main social centers of campus.

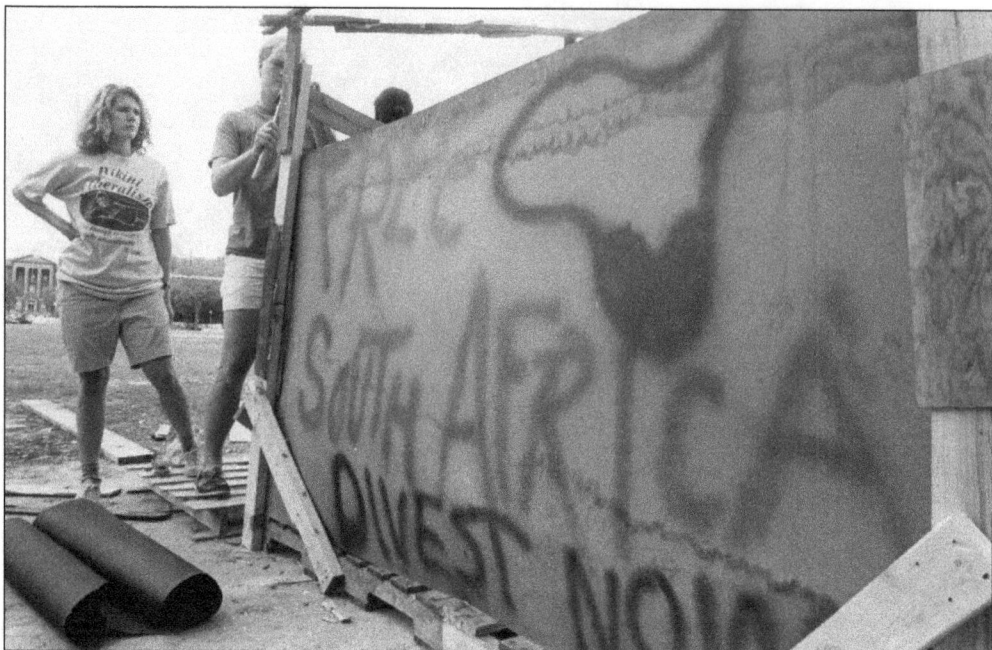

Tulane Alliance Against Apartheid built a shantytown on the University Center quad on April 21, 1988, and occupied it for five days prior to the board's meeting, hoping to convince the board to divest itself of its holdings in corporations that do business in South Africa. The board praised the students' activism but declined to take a political stand.

The Merryl and Sam Israel Jr. Environmental Sciences Building was constructed with its mission in mind. The 52,000-square-foot research center included nontoxic paints and finishes, recycled concrete and wood, recycling stations, solar-activated lighting systems, natural ventilation, and interactive sun reflectors. The building is connected to Stern Hall with a bridge. (Ann Case.)

John Giffen Weinmann's lifelong association with Tulane—Newcomb Nursery School, Arts and Sciences (bachelor of arts, 1950), Law School (bachelor of law, 1952), Medical Center Board of Governors (1969–1981) and board member (1981–1991)—was literally set in stone when, while he was board chair (1993–1998), he supported the construction of Weinmann Hall, the new home of the Law School. The building was dedicated in 1995. This view is from Monroe Hall.

The Elleonora P. McWilliams Hall was dedicated on November 21, 1996, as a new home for the Department of Theatre and Dance. The three-story building provided three dance studios on the top floor, an acting workshop space for informal performances, a costume design lab, a scene shop next to Lupin Theatre, lighting and prop storage rooms, and a computer lab for the study of scenic, costume, and lighting design. Here, students are treated to a Congolese dance class taught by Titos Sompa in 2012.

101

Under coach Tommy Bowden and quarterback Shaun King, the 1998 Tulane football team had a perfect season, winning every game it played by six or more points and setting a new single-season record for the highest number of points with 538. It did not receive a bid to play in a national title game, however, because it had not played any ranked teams and belonged to a non-BCS conference. Instead, the Green Wave played in, and won, the Liberty Bowl to end the year with a 12-0 record.

At the final commencement of the old millennium, a new president ushered in an old tradition. Scott S. Cowen presided over his first commencement ceremony, unifying all 11 schools and colleges in the Superdome for the conferring of degrees and awarding of symbolic diplomas (authentic for doctoral candidates). Cowen also debuted the President's Medal, to be awarded at the sole discretion of the president to individuals who have distinguished themselves by contributing to the well-being of the university. Cokie Roberts was its first recipient.

The first Wave Goodbye, a pre-commencement Friday-night party on Gibson quad, was held in 2000. It became an instant "must-do" event. Like a mini–Jazz Fest, it featured live music by local artists such as Irvin Mayfield, shown here in 2004. With small plates available from festival-style food booths, the celebration honored the graduates and treated their family members to a little New Orleans lagniappe.

From 1995 to 2003, the Green Wave women's basketball team was dominant in Conference-USA. Under coach Lisa Stockton, the Lady Wave earned nine consecutive invitations to the NCAA postseason tournament, making it to the second round three times. The team's best season was in 1997, when it went 27-5, won the conference regular season and tournament, and entered postseason play as the number-four seed.

In 2003, Tulane athletics faced a crisis when, despite having successful teams, the department was running an annual deficit of $7 million, in part because Conference-USA was not a member of the Bowl Championship Series, which hampered its revenue stream. It considered withdrawing from NCAA Division I-A but decided instead to challenge the unfair BCS system. President Cowen formed the Presidential Coalition for Athletics Reform; ultimately, the BCS was discarded in favor of a selection committee and playoffs for the national championship.

Under coach Rick Jones, Tulane's baseball team enjoyed a decade of success, culminating in its first ever preseason number-one ranking in 2005, and it held that spot for most of the year. It matched the 2001 team's 55 season wins, won the Conference-USA tournament, regional and super regional series (and dogpiled in celebration), and went to the College World Series in Omaha as the number-one overall seed. Unfortunately, the Green Wave was eliminated in its third game, the same fate that befell the 2001 squad. (Dave Browning.)

Four

KATRINA AND BEYOND
2005–2015

In August 2005, Tulane's world changed. Rather than presenting a traditional orientation address on freshman Move-In Day on August 27, 2005, Pres. Scott Cowen welcomed the students to campus and then kindly told them to leave. Hurricane Katrina was headed towards New Orleans, necessitating the evacuation of campus. Students who were unable to leave with their parents boarded buses to Jackson, Mississippi, to wait out the storm. Cowen stayed on campus to witness the storm and its aftermath.

After the levees broke and the city flooded, and it became clear that Tulane was in critical condition, Cowen and the university's administration convened in Houston to devise a plan through which the university could begin to function again. The Renewal Plan, designed to achieve financial viability while remaining true to the long-term goals of the university—to focus the university's resources on programs in which it had potential to excel, to offer world-class undergraduate education, and to take the lessons learned from Katrina to help rebuild New Orleans and to extend those lessons to other communities—initially drew criticism, but it ultimately enabled the university to survive and then thrive.

Academically, the major changes in the reorganization included the loss of faculty positions, the elimination of undergraduate programs from the School of Engineering, and the elimination of Newcomb College as a separate, degree-granting entity. Undergraduate students were combined into a single undergraduate college, Newcomb-Tulane College, with new on-campus residency requirements within residential colleges the first two years and with public service requirements for graduation.

Approximately 13,000 students enrolled in about 600 host colleges across the country in the fall 2005 semester. The athletic teams carried the torch, dispersed to different universities that took them in as groups. The football team played in 11 different stadiums, and the students were there to support them. Tulane reopened in January 2006 and moved forward in creating a better, more focused Tulane University.

In 2015, the last Katrina-remediated building was finally finished—two new floors were added atop the library to replace space that was no longer usable due to the possibility of flooding. The storm's 10-year anniversary was commemorated with an exhibit in the Lavin-Bernick Center that documented Tulane's remarkable recovery and highlighted its many innovations and accomplishments in the past decade.

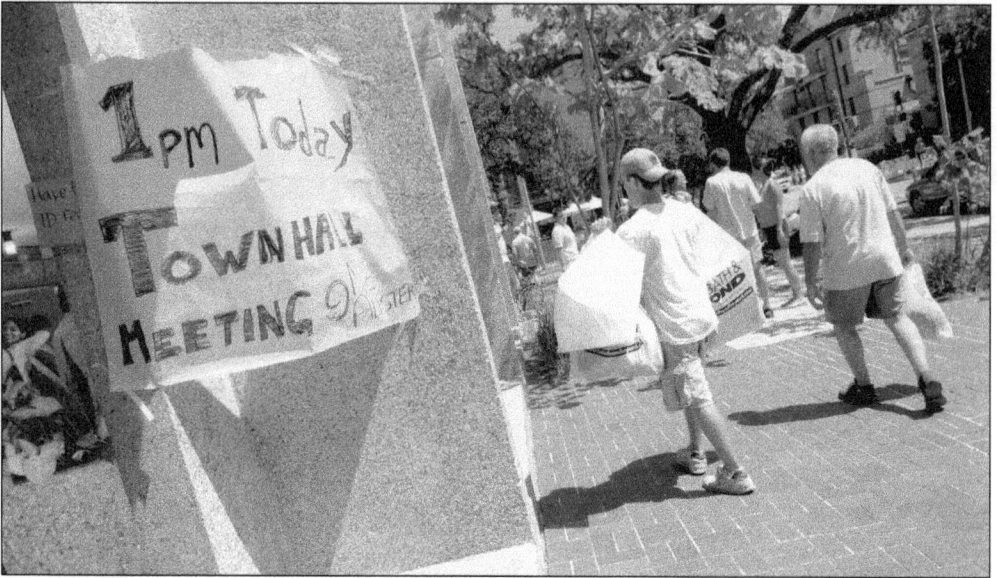

Saturday, August 27, 2005, was Move-In Day for Tulane, the day that families bring their students to campus to begin the semester. Unfortunately, it seemed that Hurricane Katrina intended to move in as well. Overnight, the hurricane's predicted path had shifted far enough to the west that it was now aimed at New Orleans. It was a category 3 storm at this time but was expected to increase in intensity.

Rather than stage a full-regalia orientation to the new students, Pres. Scott Cowen addressed the newcomers in shorts and a polo shirt, alone on stage. He appraised the students of the situation and then dismissed them, either to their homes or to be evacuated with other students to the university-appointed shelter in Jackson, Mississippi. They were sent back to their rooms to pack a small travel bag with a few days' supplies.

After the evacuating students registered with administrative staff in the Reily Recreation Center so that everyone could be accounted for, they boarded buses that were waiting to take them to Jackson State University. Several key administrators accompanied them. Once there, the 400 or so students camped on air mattresses in the gymnasium to wait out the storm. (Louis Mayer.)

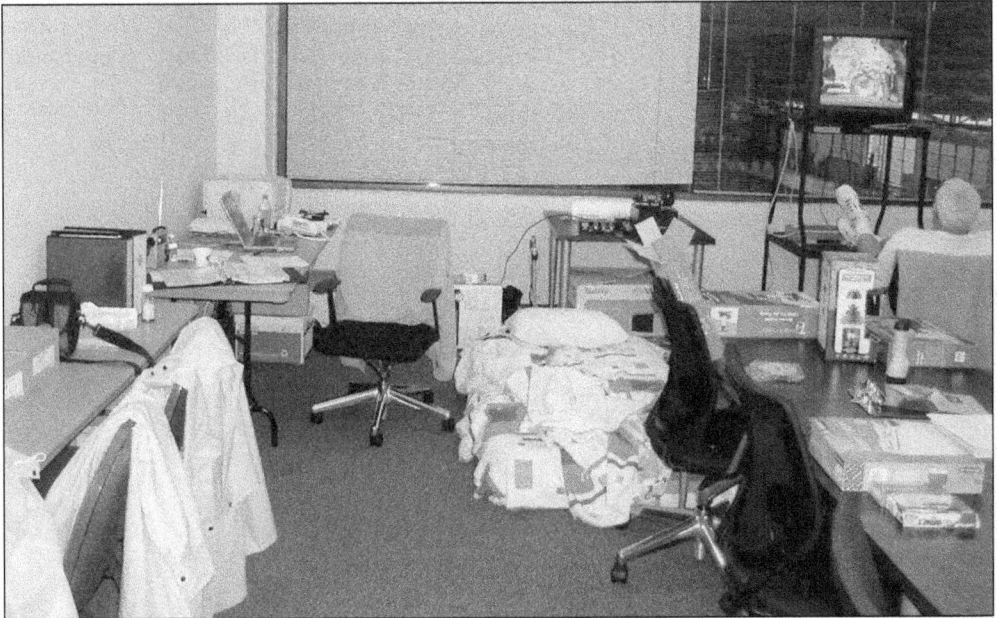

Once the students had left campus, President Cowen, director of emergency preparedness Louis Mayer, other essential administrators, and a few facilities and grounds personnel retreated to their designated bunkers to ride out the storm. Cowen monitored what was now a category 5 hurricane from the command center in Reily as it approached the Louisiana coastline on Sunday, August 28. Outside, New Orleans was put under a mandatory evacuation order.

Monday morning, August 29, Katrina's effects were felt on campus. The storm's gusts were clocked at 140 miles per hour, a category 3 storm, and they blew for 12 hours. The city lost power, but Tulane's generators were operating. After the storm passed, vice president for university communication Debbie Grant and President Cowen found that the campus had survived with an acceptable amount of damage. Because of the number of old oaks on campus and the force of the hurricane's winds, there was an extensive amount of debris on the ground, but it was not catastrophic. There was no groundwater except for rain puddles.

On Monday evening, President Cowen was informed that several levees in the city had broken. The group decided to stay another night on campus to see if Tulane would be affected; they awoke to find themselves on an island. Like the bowl to which New Orleans has always been compared, geographically speaking (since its center is so much lower than its outer edges), the city had filled up overnight. Everyone lost power, water pressure, and ability to communicate electronically beyond text message. Water stretched from the Reily Center north across the practice field to Rosen House and south down McAlister Extension as far as was visible. The most feasible mode of transportation was by boat; luckily, several boats were found and put into service. As the day wore on, other people stranded on campus were ferried to the Reily Center, raising its population to 30 people. (Both, Louis Mayer.)

With the food supply dwindling, Scott Cowen and several of the facilities workers foraged for rations in the campus buildings, breaking into Bruff Commons for the largest stash. Fuel for the motorboats was also obtained where it could be found. It was hot, with highs in the 90s. The castaways spent their nights on the roof of the Reily Center, where they had fresh air, and waited. By Wednesday, August 31, equilibrium had been reached, and the water stopped rising. Exploring by man-lift, Cowen and others found that the floodwaters stood up to six feet deep in spots on campus. It turned the quads from Newcomb to McAlister into a lake. Meanwhile, in Jackson, the storm had knocked out electricity; the students had to be evacuated a second time, sent back to their homes on Thursday. (Above, Louis Mayer.)

With the students safely dispatched to their homes, Scott Cowen and the other administrators finally left campus on Thursday, September 1, to join the rest of the administration at an outpost office established in Houston by Anne Baños. To get there, they traveled by boat to Freret Street, which was the extent of the flooding, then by golf cart to St. Charles Avenue, then by dump truck to the levee, where a helicopter was waiting for them. The Facilities Services crew stayed at Reily to do what it could to clean campus when the water receded and to help in the neighborhood. Four days after Katrina, National Guardsmen arrived in the city to patrol; some of them bunked in Gibson Hall and on the quads.

Across the lake at the Primate Center, pre-storm preparations had proved sufficient. The center suffered a loss of electricity, telephone, cell phone, and internet service, but had not flooded. Many roads were impassable due to downed trees. However, the buildings suffered remarkably little damage. In New Orleans, at the downtown campuses of Tulane, the situation was much the same as it was at the uptown campus. The damage to the buildings was something that could be fixed. What could not be salvaged, perhaps, was the years' worth of research stored in frozen biological specimens that would be lost due to the extended power outage and the three-foot-high floodwaters that permeated the first-floor offices. (Above, Mike Aertker; below, Dr. Tracy Conrad.)

At the Tulane University Hospital and Clinic, the rising floodwaters threatened to douse the generators, cutting off the power to seven critical patients on ventilators. Another hospital said that it would accept the patients if they could be evacuated, but Tulane's hospital had no boat and no helipad. To enable evacuation by air, hospital maintenance staff removed four light poles from the rooftop parking deck of the nearby garage so that helicopters could land. Then each patient was carried down to the second-floor walkway and through the walkway to the garage, put into the bed of a pickup truck, driven up six floors to the roof, and loaded into a helicopter. Later, less critical patients were evacuated by watercraft with assistance from the Louisiana Department of Wildlife and Fisheries. (Both, Dr. Tracy Conrad.)

The administration reassembled in Houston and immediately began to make hard decisions. First, it canceled the fall semester, becoming the only major research university to cancel a full semester since the Civil War. Then it announced that Tulane students would be accepted at other institutions for the semester. Concerned about its inability to communicate with staff because the email system was inoperable, it created an online register so that staff members could log in, and it updated an emergency website with daily news. It also assured staff members that paychecks would continue, at least for the immediate future. (Both, Mary Mouton.)

Facilities Services' grounds department was called back to campus as soon as the water began to recede around mid-September. Those who could make it back returned to a city with few support services. Often living on MREs (Meals Ready-To-Eat) and water distributed by the Red Cross and the National Guard, and having to pass through security checks to drive onto campus, they began the laborious task of gathering and hauling off 600 cubic yards of downed limbs, repairing or replacing flooded tools and machinery, and restoring the campus to its former beauty, all while facing a second weather-related threat when Hurricane Rita blew by on September 24.

President Cowen sent the athletic teams out en masse to one of five universities in Texas and Louisiana, tasked "to carry the torch, be the face, and represent the name" of Tulane as they competed. The football team was put to the test, having been evacuated from Jackson, Mississippi, to Dallas, Texas, and then landing at Louisiana Tech University to live in a dorm that was scheduled to be demolished. Playing 11 games in 11 different stadiums, it won two games, narrowly losing two others. Above, the Wave beat Southeastern Louisiana University, playing in Baton Rouge on October 1. Wherever the team played, students were there to support it; the photograph below was taken at the game against Houston the following week, played in Lafayette, Louisiana. For its perseverance, the team was presented with the Disney Wide World of Sports Spirit Award and the 2005 Courage Award by the Football Writers Association of America and the FedEx Orange Bowl.

Uptown, Howard-Tilton Memorial Library and Jones Hall, the special collections library, both suffered heavily when floodwaters rose in their basements. Eight feet of water in Howard-Tilton submerged more than 700,000 print volumes and recordings and nearly 1.5 million pieces of microfiche and microfilm. In Jones Hall, four feet of water affected another 700,000 manuscript folders in archival boxes. Belfor, a disaster management company, was called in to retrieve the wet volumes and documents, freeze them, remediate them, and ultimately return the salvaged items to the library's collections. The Tulane Library Recoveries Center processed the returned material. Approximately 300,000 volumes and 630,000 archival items were treated and returned. The remaining items in the libraries were saved from being damaged by mold by large tubes that pumped dry air into each building. (Both, Andy Corrigan.)

Through the gracious assistance of almost 600 different host institutions, 13,000 Tulane students attended classes across the country during the fall 2005 semester. Boston College enrolled 320 undergraduates, Baylor University welcomed 400 Tulane medical students and faculty, and almost 200 students and faculty spent the semester at Cornell. The students in this photograph chose Princeton for their unscripted semester in exile, where they visited Paul Tulane's grave. (Caleb M.X. Dance.)

In order to entice faculty, staff, and students to return to the broken city to work, there had to be someplace for them to live and schools for their children to attend. Hence Tulane bought an apartment building, rented a cruise ship to serve as housing, and chartered a local elementary school for children of both the university and the general public. Lusher Elementary is just a few blocks from campus.

On campus, Belfor's recovery teams spent months going into each of the buildings, stripping them of everything that had gotten wet. Items that could be sanitized of toxic mold were salvaged; everything else was discarded. Another company followed the repair work with environmental remediation to ensure that the buildings were again safe for occupation. The image above shows refrigerators being discarded out of the Willow Residences; the image below illustrates the loss of office records due to the flooding. The cost of recovery to the university was $650 million, a portion of which was covered through insurance and FEMA reimbursement.

The School of Architecture created the Tulane City Center, opened on November 14, 2005, as an urban outreach and research program in which faculty and students work together to design and construct projects to help with the rebuilding of the city, especially in the nonprofit sector. In the URBANbuild program, students received hands-on experience designing and building houses for low-income families, learning framing and carpentry.

Tulane University—A Plan for Renewal

The unprecedented nature and scope of Hurricane Katrina presented Tulane University with unprecedented challenges. In the aftermath, Tulane's administration and board were faced immediately with securing the survival and recovery of the institution. But for Tulane, survival and recovery were not the finishing line, merely where to begin the most serious undertaking in the history of the university—developing the plan that would ensure the continuing academic ascendancy and financial health of Tulane University.

It took Tulane 172 years to become one of the most respected and highly regarded universities in the nation, and the university's leadership pledged, rather than allow disaster to destroy Tulane's legacy and dream of world-class academic excellence, instead the university would redefine and renew itself for the future.

The plan that evolved is predicated on defining Tulane University by four characteristics:

o The renewed Tulane University will be defined by its world-class educational and research programs.
o Tulane will be defined by its unique relationship to the culturally rich and diverse city of New Orleans, which is characterized by one of the world's great waterways and serves as a gateway to the Americas.
o Tulane will be defined by its historical strengths and ability to strategically redefine itself in light of an unprecedented natural disaster in ways that will ultimately benefit the Tulane community, New Orleans and other communities around the globe.
o Tulane will be defined by its financial strength and vitality.

At the center of the renewed Tulane will be an exceptional undergraduate program that is campus- and student-centric, and dedicated to the holistic development of

The Renewal Plan, announced on December 8, 2005, was Tulane's roadmap back from the edge of disaster. It was a sweeping reorganization that focused on the academic mission while strategically addressing its current and future operations in the post-Katrina environment. Enhancing the undergraduate experience by making it more campus-centric while addressing the $200-million budget shortfall created by recovery costs, it required the combining and/or elimination of some academic and athletic programs as well as staffing reductions.

The Lady Wave basketball team became the first athletic team of collegiate or professional level to compete in New Orleans since Katrina when it took to the court on December 18, 2005. Tulane defeated Central Connecticut State 72-60. The university had offered free tickets to anyone wishing to attend; about 800 spectators enjoyed the game. The basketball team stayed at Texas Tech University during the fall semester.

Tulane happily reopened its doors to students on January 17, 2006. At the long-delayed convocation, President Cowen began his address with the phrase, "As I was going to say before Katrina interrupted me . . . " Along with 1,342 returning Tulanians, students from Xavier and Dillard also attended classes, since their campuses had been severely damaged by the storm.

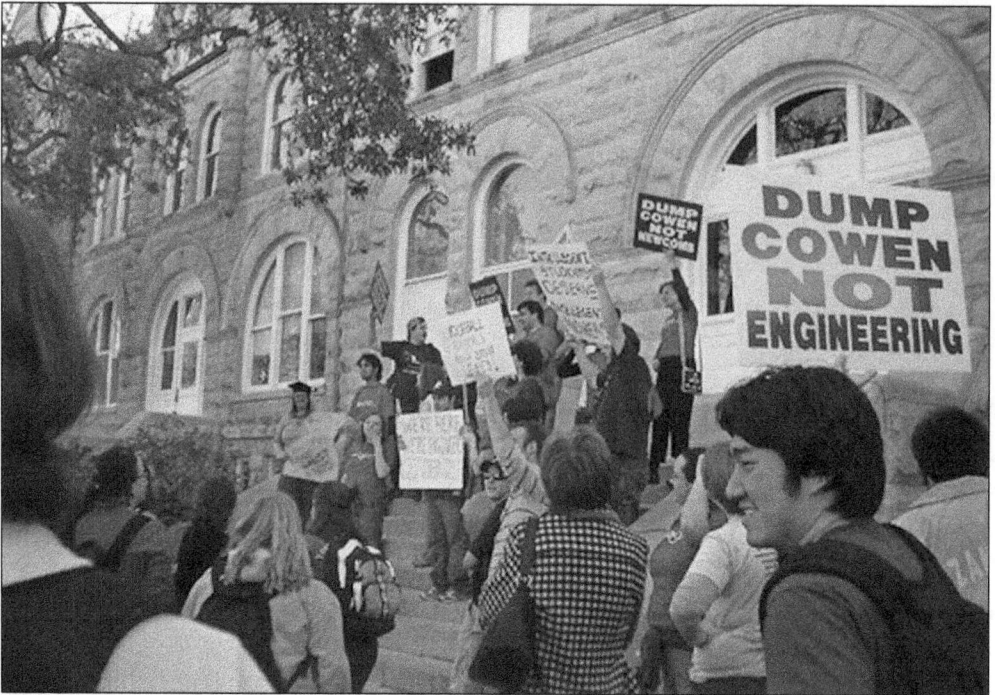
The School of Engineering was hit hard by the Renewal Plan. As part of the reorganization into the School of Science and Engineering, its departments of computer science and civil, electrical, mechanical, environmental, and computer engineering were phased out by June 2007. Students and alumni protested, but the cuts went forward as planned. (Max Berde.)

Newcomb alumnae protested the board's decision to discontinue the coordinate college system that included Newcomb College as a separate entity. Despite the establishment of the Newcomb College Institute to ensure continued emphasis on providing leadership and educational programming for women, a lawsuit was brought against Tulane claiming that the closure of Newcomb College violated the donor's intent. A five-year legal battle was waged that was ultimately decided in favor of Tulane. (NAVL.)

The Lavin-Bernick Center for University Life, better known as the LBC, was built on the bones of the old University Center. While it retained some of the same named features (Der Rathskellar and the Kendall Cram Room), it was 50 percent larger, modern, and energy-efficient. It was designed with environmentally friendly features, such as water walls for cooling and electric lights that automatically adjust depending on the amount of outside light.

The highlight of an emotional roller-coaster year was having two former US presidents as speakers at commencement in 2006. In addressing the students, both Bill Clinton, left, and George H.W. Bush praised the students for their commitment to helping rebuild the university and the city. President Cowen presented both men with honorary doctorates of law. Because the Superdome was still undergoing repair, the unified ceremony was held in the arena, giving the event a more intimate aura.

To facilitate the new public service graduation requirement, the Center for Public Service was established in August 2006. With community engagement and service-learning as key concepts for the post-Katrina student, the center functioned as a liaison between faculty, students, and community organizations. It cosponsored Outreach Tulane, the university's largest annual community service event, held one Saturday each September.

Crawfest is a student-run music, food, and arts festival created jointly by the Associated Student Body and the Residential Hall Association to have an annual event that mirrors the fall semester's homecoming. On Crawfest Saturday, 20,000 pounds of crawfish, corn, and potatoes are served while bands play on the quads between Newcomb Hall and McAlister Auditorium.

124

Weatherhead Hall was the second (after Wall) of the residences to be built in the residential college system. Opened in August 2011, it has 269 beds configured in 144 suites of single- and double-occupancy rooms. It is located on the site of the former Old Doris and New Doris women's dormitories. The hall was originally scheduled to begin construction on August 29, 2005, the day that Katrina struck.

The Barbara Greenbaum House at Newcomb Lawn was the most recent residential college to open on campus, in August 2014. Housing 256 students in 144 rooms, it was themed as a Get Engaged Living Learning Community; residents committed to participating in at least one Living Learning Community–specific activity each month. The residence is located on Zimpel Street at Broadway Street, between Newcomb Chapel and the Boot. (Ann Case.)

The Donna and Paul Flower Hall for Research and Innovation opened in 2012 as a contemporary space that bridges academia and industry. The 24,000-square-foot building includes a modernized Francis Taylor Laboratory. Designed to encourage collaboration between faculty and students, it hosts the Phyllis M. Taylor Center for Social Innovation and Design Thinking. (Jackson Hill.)

Two new floors were added to the top of Howard-Tilton Memorial Library to replace space lost in the basements of Jones Hall and the library itself. This FEMA-funded build-back project took eight years to complete, and put to rest the campus legend that the library had originally been designed to carry two extra floors, but had been capped at four floors because the weight of the additional floors and books would cause the building to sink. (Ann Case.)

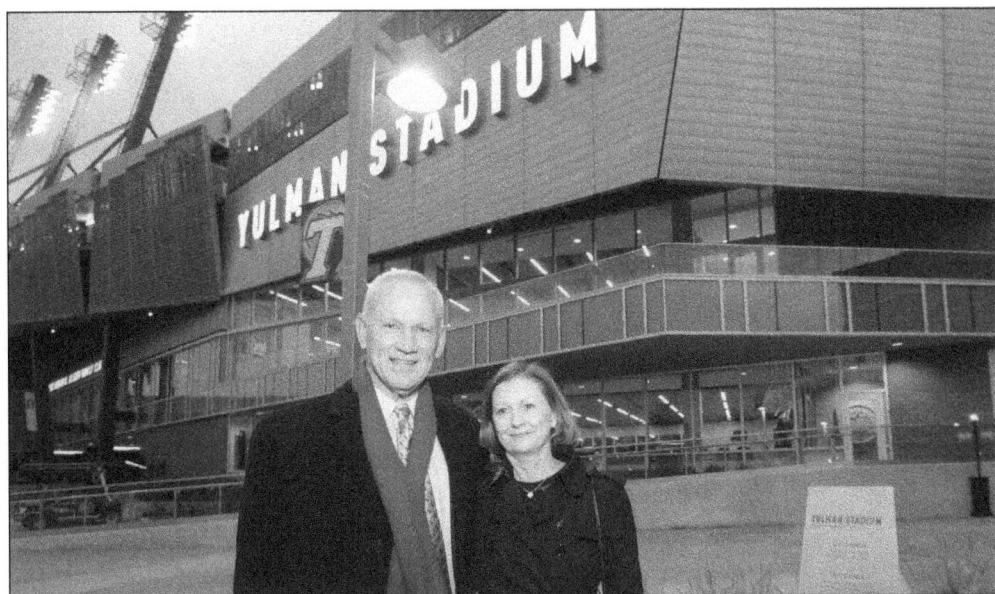

For many, Yulman Stadium represented the crowning glory of capital projects completed after Katrina. In bringing football back to campus after 40 years, it supported the Renewal Plan's goal to be more campus-centric and enhanced the undergraduate experience in drawing students together. Athletic director Rick Dickson, executive vice president for university relations and development Yvette Jones, and president emeritus Scott Cowen, not shown, were honored for making the stadium a reality. (Tracie Morris Schaefer.)

Named for benefactors Richard and Janet Yulman, with facilities donated by the Benson and Glazer families, Yulman Stadium sits in the general area of the previous Tulane Stadium but is only one-third its size. Tailgating on the Newcomb and LBC quads precedes home games, and the Tulane University Marching Band leads the crowd from the quad to the stadium at game time. Roll Wave! (Jackson Hill.)

127

Visit us at
arcadiapublishing.com

www.ingramcontent.com/pod-product-compliance
Lightning Source LLC
Chambersburg PA
CBHW050704150426
42813CB00055B/2451

* 9 7 8 1 5 3 1 6 9 9 0 9 3 *